Table Of Contents

Introduction 3
Chapter 1: Using Your Emotions as A Tool 7
Chapter 2: Confidence Is Key 19
Chapter 3: Finding the Right Partner 28
Chapter 4: Attracting Other People 36
Chapter 5: Navigating Online Dating 44
Chapter 6: Some Dating Tips You'll Actually Use 53
Chapter 7: Maintaining the Relationship You Worked For.... 62
Chapter 8: Applying All This to Real Life 70
Chapter 9: Having Fun with It All 74
Conclusion 76

Introduction	80
Chapter 1 - The Prison of Fear	83
Chapter 2 - Opportunity	87
Chapter 3 – Change	92
Chapter 4 – Growing Yourself	100
Chapter 5 – Be Realistic and Honest with Yourself	110
Chapter 6 – Choose Your Friends Wisely	113
Section 2: Hints, Tips and Techniques	118
Chapter 7: The Strength of a Smile	118
Chapter 8 – Nonverbal Cues	126
Chapter 9 – The Metre Rule	132
Chapter 10 – Asking Effective Questions	139
Chapter 11 – The Secret Recipe	147
Chapter 12 – Lifelong Learning and Development	151
Bonus	154

DATING FOR WOMEN PLAYBOOK

Transformational Dating Advice For Women Including How To Achieve Better Relationships, Effortlessly Attract More Men, Online Dating Tips & Tinder Secrets To Boost Your Self-Esteem

By Matthew Stone & Julie Hussey

© 2018

©Copyright 2018 – All rights reserved

The contents of this book may not be reproduced, duplicated or transmitted without direct written permission from the author.

Under no circumstances will any legal responsibility or blame be held against the author or publisher for any reparation, damage or monetary loss due to the information herein, either directly or indirectly.

Legal Notice

This book is copyright protected. This is for personal use only. You cannot amend, distribute, sell, use, quote or paraphrase any part of the content in this book without written consent from the author.

Disclaimer Notice

Please note that the information contained within this document is for educational and entertainment purposes only. Every attempt has been made to provide accurate, up to date and reliable information. No warranties of any kind are expressed or implied. Readers acknowledge that the author is not engaging the rendering of legal, financial, medical or professional advice. The content of this book has been derived from various sources. Please consult a licensed professional before attempting any techniques outlined in this book.

By reading this document, the reader agrees that under no circumstance is the author responsible for any losses, direct or indirect, that are incurred as a result of the use of the information contained within this document, including – but not limited to – errors, omissions or inaccuracies.

Introduction

The goal after reading this book is for women to feel intensely empowered. This can be done once your perspective on the dating world and men in general changes. Once the secrets of dating have been uncovered and learned by you as the reader, your life will completely change. It won't be long before men are knocking at your door, begging to date you. Not only will the dates increase, but the ability to maintain positive and healthy relationships with your suitors will become stronger as well. If you're ready to find your Mr. Right, have him fall hard for you, and spend the rest of your life living out your dream, this is the place to start!

It all begins with changing your perception on dating as a whole. It doesn't matter if you're freshly single from a long marriage or a committed relationship. Maybe you've never dated in your life and are ready to start. Perhaps you've been trying to find the right one for an endless amount of time with no luck. Women of all shapes, sizes, colours, and everything in between can find their happily ever after by starting off with this book. It's all already inside of you, and we're here to help make sure you find what it takes to fulfil your dating fantasies.

When you see couples that seem mismatched, or a partner that seems unattractive, you might wonder what it is about the two that made them fall for each other. There are some women that seem to have every man in the world vying for their attention, and others that seem to have it all, but no men have any interest in them. It might make you wonder, what is it about these women that the other women are lacking?

It comes natural to some women, and others need to practice and study to become the most desirable. It starts with the manipulation of the male mind, and once this technique is mastered, it can feel like a superpower.

In this book, we're going to break down for you what these powers are and how you can take them and apply them to your everyday life. Not every woman will learn of these powers and figure out how to use them. They might still get dates and have relationships, but in the end, they might be more likely to face heartbreak.

It can be easy to become a bitter woman, broken down by men and heartbreak. Maybe there's one guy that you just can't seem to get out of your head. He might hurt you, but there's something about him that keeps you coming back. Maybe there was just one guy that messed everything up and made it difficult for you to open yourself up and love again. There are plenty of men that are cheaters, liars, and overall douchebags.

Surprisingly, we believe that not all men are like this. It can be hard to come to terms with that, but in reality, there are plenty of amazing men out there that are ready to make you theirs! It's not about luck, chance, or just finding the right man waiting for you on your doorstep. The key is understanding what makes a good man and being able to pick them out of a crowd. More importantly is being the type of woman that that good man wants to be faithful and dedicated to. This is the challenging part, but the powers we go over in the book will help you get there.

The more you know, the more powerful you can become. This is what you've been waiting for, and everything is about to change. Instead of getting your heart broken, you're the one that's going to be doing the breaking. It can be scary to risk it all, but in the end, it might be the most exciting thing you'll ever do.

We've broken the book into nine parts for you. In each of these parts, we're going to discuss the essential ideas necessary to achieve your dating goals. Think of it like a 'Dating Playbook' It's encouraged to take notes throughout the book, so you can see some examples, arguments, and other helpful tips that you can apply to your everyday life. Revisiting these ideas will only help grow your knowledge, which, in turn, will grow your power.

Just a warning before you get into the book, it might not be for everyone. There are going to be moments of brutal honesty, bluntness, and other things that aren't easy to hear. It might be scary but confronting these challenges will only make you stronger in the end.

This isn't about being delicate, because that's not what's in store for you in the dating world. It's time to be realistic with yourself and the world, but that doesn't have to be a bad thing. You just have to be willing to confront yourself. You're going to have to dig deep inside your mind, soul, and body. If you stay committed to this book and your dreams of a better dating life, it will happen for you. Most importantly, you have to be ready for a change. A big one.

There's a reason why you're reading this book. You've already come into this with a predisposed image on men and dating. That has to change. Don't worry, you won't be doing it all on your own. We're here to help. We can't do everything, however. You have to be the one that's willing to jump in the deep end, no matter how cold the water might be.

It can be uncomfortable to apply these ideas to your real life, but that's what it's all about. Normal isn't comfortable, and your normal hasn't been working thus far, so it's time to change things up. It's time to be brave, willing to change, and ready for the future. It'll take practice, but everything does. Nothing's going to happen overnight. You're not going to finish the book and instantly get a text or knock on your door from a man. It's not easy, but this book will give you all the tools you need to find the person you've been looking for.

The first step, even before starting the first chapter, is to open yourself up. Leave behind all the other ideas you've had about men and dating and start fresh today. The experiences you've had are certainly important, but don't let them define you anymore. Once you're able to do that and take the tools we give you in this book, you'll be able to find The One, and never let another man make you hurt.

So, without further ado, let's get started!

Chapter 1: Using Your Emotions as A Tool

Emotions come naturally to us, so of course, it's going to be challenging to learn to use and manipulate your own feelings to your advantage. That's why we put this chapter first. If you can conquer your own emotions, you'll be able to breeze through the rest of the book with ease.

Women are known for being the more emotional of the sexes, men being the more sexually driven. That's why it can be so challenging to control your emotions. We're wired to listen to them. They're ingrained in our bodies for protection and healing. Men have them too, but in the dating world, it seems their sexual desire takes rank. It doesn't matter where you're from, this will likely remain true. We all look different and act opposite on the outside, but on the inside, we have the same innerworkings, the same wires that are biologically placed.

Don't deny your own natural instincts. It's not about turning off your emotions. If you did that, you wouldn't be human anymore. Our ability to think and feel so deeply is a tool that allows us to be great mothers, lovers, sisters, and friends.

Get the idea that emotional equals weak out of your head ASAP. Everyone has emotions, and women just happen to feel them a bit more. This by no means proves that women are weak in any way. They are actually stronger because of them, but our patriarchal society would have you feeling otherwise. We're not asking you to lose all emotion. Just learn how to control them and use them to your advantage rather than allowing them to be your weakness.

Once you gain power over your emotions, you'll also gain power over men. Men have been using our emotions against us for far too long. They call you weak, whiny, moody, and anything else they can to make you feel as though your emotions are wrong. These words are meant to hurt you, but you should allow them to make you feel more powerful.

It's time for a new normal. We can easily let ourselves fall into relationships that are unhealthy just because it's normal. Maybe you saw your mother or friend in a bad relationship, and now you're in one yourself, all because it's what seems normal. Normal isn't always right, and we're here to help you really flip the switch and take back charge of your emotions.

Men Are Already in Control of Your Emotions

You're reading this because you want to figure men out. What you need to know, is that there are some men already have a pretty decent grasp on our emotions. Men have been manipulating us, lying and cheating for centuries. That's because they're able to logically look at our emotions and use them as our weaknesses.

Some men don't even realize what they're doing. Women make it too easy for men and allow them to take a part of themselves and turn it around, only to have it used against them. There are still plenty of men that know exactly what they're doing, and these are the most dangerous kinds. It's best to just avoid these men, but, if you do run into one, we hope you'll have the tools to take control.

While there are plenty of Prince Charming's in the world, there are still plenty of men that can be dangerous when it comes to using your own emotions against you. They can manipulate your feelings to exactly what they want, which includes money, sex, or maybe just a place to stay. Men are good at this, but it's time for women to be even better.

Of course, not all men are like this. When we talk about men, we're speaking on the general population, but it's important for you to not look at every single man as someone you should conquer. That doesn't mean you can't be prepared should you come face to face with someone that might try to manipulate you.

Some men, or people in general, will use you up and take everything you have, but only if you let them. They'll take every part of you to get what you want, so when they leave, of course you're going to follow! They took who you were and changed it into someone that they wanted, someone they could use. Once they're done and have had their way, you feel lost and lonely. Before it gets to this point, you have to control your emotions, so they never get to take a piece of you in the first place.

We've become bullseyes because of our own emotions. We do some silly and stupid things sometimes all in the name of our emotions. We all have that person in our past that we think about now and wonder how it lasted as long as it did. How often do you see someone you dated, wishing so badly you hadn't given them a part of you? Our emotions can cause us to do silly things, but they can also make us incredibly powerful.

Differentiate listening to your heart and head. This is one of the most important steps in controlling your emotions. We've heard it all the time, but it's true! Your heart is telling you what it thinks you want to hear. It's easy to follow your heart. Listen to your head!

Let's think of this in a logical scenario. We all know that one guy, whether you dated them, or a friend did, that was just an absolutely terrible partner. Maybe he was selfish, a slob, or a lying cheat. Either way, there's something about him that just makes him awful, but he still ended up taking control of your or your friend's heart.

Once the relationship ended, it's very clear to see that logically, you should never ever go back to that man. When it comes to your heart, however, it's going to tell you to run right back to him. This is because our hearts are hurting. They're doing what they think is right to mend the problem. You're going to run back into his arms and it'll feel great! But only for a moment. Our brain knows what's best. It's going to hurt, but you have to do what's right and just walk away.

The Emotional End of a Relationship

One of the hardest things you'll have to face when entering the dating world is accepting the end of a relationship. Breakups are hard, and no one is going to argue with that. Some of us might find the right one on our first date, and others go through more breakups than an entire group of women combined. Either way, breaking up is going to be hard to do.

You might want to follow your emotions in an attempt to feel better, but you have to look at this logically. Like we already discussed, your heart is used to something normal. When your heart feels pain, its biological response is to make the pain go away. It seems as though going back to the norm is what's going to fix everything, but we have to resist that urge.

Your emotions can make you stupid. How many girls do you know that were so desperate to get back with someone they did something completely crazy? There are going to be emotions at the end of a relationship, and you might have the urge to do things you would never do otherwise. Just remind yourself that this is your heart speaking. We're going to teach you how to better listen to your head.

Identifying and Governing Your Responses

Actually, recognizing your emotions can be rather easy. It can be simple to know if you're sad, depressed, hopeless, or whatever other emotion you might be feeling. It's common for people to be sad after a breakup. Perhaps you might even feel a little relief. Along with the sadness of what was lost, you're going to feel anxiety as well. Did I make the right choice? Did I just mess everything up? That's our brain's natural reaction, and that's completely fine.

The hard part is determining how to control your reaction. The emotions aren't the problem. It's what you do with those emotions that can really make things go sour. You're going to be sad, and you're going to want to call him after a breakup. Being sad isn't wrong! But calling him is! It's important to know that you're not at fault for feeling bad, but you are for being weak and picking up the phone even though you know you shouldn't.

You have to be strong. This is where the willpower really comes in. Patience is the most important part of a breakup. If you broke your leg, you wouldn't expect to go running the next day, right? Try and treat your heart the same way.

Accepting is another challenging part. You must accept that you are going to feel pain. You are going to hurt. Unfortunately, there's just no way to avoid this. You're human! If you learn how to handle this pain, however, instead of allowing that hurt to keep you glued to your bed, you can learn how to use it as a tool to thrive.

Mending Your Broken Heart

Distraction is one of the greatest tools when it comes to fixing what was broken. If only we could just use some scotch tape or glue to help us feel better when we've fallen apart. Our hearts and brains don't work that way. Instead, distraction is a key part in moving on.

You're going to think about him. There's no eraser for memories or way to block out certain thoughts. Even if there were, that's not the healthy way to handle things! When you're with friends, maybe you hear a song that reminds you of him. Maybe he was so important in your life that even the sidewalk you're stepping on causes you to think of him! This is normal, but don't let it control you. Don't let your emotions do something that you'll regret.

It's going to be painful, but distraction will help. The more you can keep your mind off of your ex, the easier it will be to move on. If you don't let your mind wander to the dark corners of your brain, you won't be asking yourself those anxiety-inducing questions such as, does he still love me? Did I do the right thing?

The pain will dissolve. It might never go away, just like a broken bone will never heal the exact way it was in the beginning. This doesn't mean your leg isn't good anymore! It's just different now, but in a way, it can be even stronger!

A Quick Guide for Controlling Emotions

1. Emotions are natural. Remember that you are not at fault for the way you feel. It's OK to be sad, angry, and emotional.
2. Don't let your emotions dictate. It's perfectly fine to feel the way you feel, but the key is how you let your feelings control your actions.
3. Accept that you will feel pain. This is inevitable. You can't have the good without the bad first, but trust me, the good will be worth it in the end.
4. You are in control! It might feel like you're falling down a hole with no grip but remember that it's your mind. Your heart. Your brain. You're in charge, even in the times you don't feel that way.
5. Let yourself heal. Don't put yourself down because you're still thinking of him. Don't force yourself into more painful situations. It's time to heal, and that's OK.
6. Distraction is key! The more you keep your mind occupied, the less of a chance that it'll trick you into doing something stupid and based on your emotions and anxieties.

Don't Give the Man Anymore Power

You're going to want to check his social media. You might even drive or walk by where he works or lives. This is normal. Everyone has the desire to see what's going on with the person that took a piece of you. Those are your emotions. Your emotional state will make you want to do those silly things. Now it's time to control them. You're in charge. You decide if you're actually going to do that.

The pain will be there but direct it towards something else! It's normal to want to become a private investigator of your ex after things have ended. It's going to hurt, and you might think that seeing what they're up to will help make you feel better. It might, but just for a moment. Stay strong, patient, and accepting. Understand that it's going to take time, and don't let that man take anymore of your time than you've already given him.

The Greatest Distractions to Mend Your Heart

As we've already discussed, you're going to need to distract yourself. When a baby's crying, the first thing a mom might do is distract it with something shiny. Eventually, the baby forgets why it was crying in the first place! It might seem silly, but the same can be said about our emotions! We were all babies at one point, after all. We're going to share with you some distractions that'll help mend your broken heart.

Practice Dates

Dating is the best way to start the healing process. It seems counterintuitive. Remember, though, when you're hungover, sometimes the best cure is to have a drink of the same thing that made you sick in the first place! The last thing you're going to want to do is date again but getting out there and meeting new people is the best way to do it. Don't be afraid to ask for help! Maybe your friends know someone they can at least set you up with for a blind date.

You're going to think about your ex. In some cases, probably more than you think about the person sitting across from you. It's going to be hard the first, second, or third date. But eventually, you'll get back to your old self and realize the importance of meeting new people.

You don't have to commit yourself to every date. If you're on dating apps, which obviously you should be at this point, you probably get messages or at least see people you would never think to date. Why not try to use them as your practice dates? Who knows, maybe this person you never saw yourself with could actually be the one! And if they're not, at least you can't say you didn't at least try. Sometimes, when you have nothing to lose is when you gain the most.

The worst thing that could happen is that you have a boring time. That's OK! You never have to go out with them again! At least you can get a free meal from it, or maybe a funny story to share with friends later that night. It can feel wrong, knowing that you might not be fully committed to this person, but it's just a first date. How do you know that they're not doing the same thing?

Trust me, the men won't walk away being hurt. Half of them are just hoping to get into a bed for the night, but you don't have to worry about that. It's not your responsibility to make sure that the men are getting what they want. This is your turn, your time. Go out and have fun. There's no pressure for commitment, and in the end, you might make a new friend. The most important thing is to just keep yourself distracted.

Men have used women for so long, it's our turn now. Use these dates to figure out what you do and don't want. Build your confidence and realize you have what it takes to be that flirty and bubbly girl you've always envied. Now's your chance to practice conversations and see what works and what doesn't. It'll be scary at first, but in the end, so worth it.

Practice dates are one of the most important tools you'll have. It's not only a distraction, but one step further to taking power over your life.

Write A Letter to Your Ex

We know, we know. Up until this point, we've told you to cut off all contact with your ex. Now we're asking you to write a letter? Well, whatever you choose to write isn't meant for them to read, only you. Grab a pen and piece of paper and write down everything you don't like about them. Write down the things they did or said to make you mad and sad. Write down even the small stuff, like their breath smelled or their nose was too big. Nothing is off limits.

Writing down everything you loathed about the other person is your chance to really reclaim yourself. Once you're done with the letter or list, it's time for you to decide what to do. Maybe you could rip it up and throw it into the lake. Perhaps you could set it on fire with all the other things that remind you of your ex. Some might choose to keep the letter around as a reminder when they're missing the person they wrote the letter about.

These tools will help anyone and everyone who's in the dating world. It's a distraction for you and a reminder of everything wrong with that relationship. When we're separated from that, it can be easy to only remember the good things. There's a reason it didn't work out in the first place, and your letter will help remind you of that.

Your Emotions as A Weapon in The Beginning

So far, we've discussed the importance of controlling your emotions after a breakup. The struggle doesn't stop there. It's important to take control of your emotions again once you've started dating again as well. Just as easily as your emotions could make you do something silly after a breakup, they could do some damage in the beginning as well.

When you meet someone you really like, of course, you're going to want to call and text them immediately. Don't! Use that same willpower you used in your last breakup now. Put down the phone and let them come to you. Of course, you don't want to completely ignore them, but there's a fine line between being desperate and being cold. You have to find that balance, and it starts with self-control.

The Most Important Reasons to Practice Self Control

1. If you confuse him, he'll only work harder. Men don't like feeling powerless. If you're desperate and needy right away, they know they have all the power. Keep yourself cool and collected, and he'll come to you. You'll leave him confused and wondering if he likes you rather than the other way around.
2. Men are natural hunters. They like a challenge and they want what they can't have. Men like it even more if you don't seem interested, as it's a challenge they can overcome. Of course, not all men are like this, but if you go into a relationship knowing the man is going to want a challenge, you'll end up coming out on top.
3. Rushing can cause more breakage. Your heart is fragile. You wouldn't just going throwing it around if you could hold it, would you? Take things slow so as to not allow yourself to become a victim of a broken heart again. Remember, don't get too cold, but if you practice self-control, reasons 1 and 2 come naturally to you.

How Can I Tell If He Likes Me?

Does he like me? That question can be the most stressful one you'll ask, but it can also be rather exciting. All men are different, but at the core, they share a lot of similarities. If he likes you, he's going to make it work.

Don't let yourself be the pursuer. He might be shy, but if he really likes you, if he really can't get you out of his head, he's still going to be the one to make the first move. If he doesn't put in the effort to get your attention in the first place, it's a warning sign of how much effort he'd put into the relationship.

Patience is the most important. When guys get flirty, you're instantly going to think they like you. Don't give in right away. Make him work for it!

Don't be afraid to flirt! Yes, some think it's better to wait for men to come to you, but there might be some that take a little more reassurance before they make a move. If you're flirty, this is a way to let him know that you're there and ready for some dedication. At the very least, flirting is always good practice.

If it never happens, maybe it's meant to be. Maybe he's been hurt, or maybe he's too shy to make a move. If he really likes, and really sees what makes you special, he'll work hard to get your attention. If not, there are plenty of other guys out there willing to put the work in.

Learn to take a hint. Sometimes, you just have to accept that he's not the one. It can be hard, especially if you've already invested time. Unfortunately, you have to use that patience and acceptance we've discussed to know when it's time to move onto the next.

STAY STRONG!

We've covered a lot so far, and you might start to feel a little overwhelmed. If you do, that's great! Like we said, this isn't going to be easy. You should feel a little overloaded, but don't worry, we're not done yet. This isn't easy but finding The One will be the greatest thing you'll ever do.

The most important thing for you to do is to take charge. You're in control! Emotions are not easy. Everyone has them, and everyone uses them in different ways. It's important that you use yours for empowerment, and don't let others see them as a weakness.

The same weapons used against you for so long are now yours to reclaim.

Chapter 2: Confidence Is Key

Once you achieve a high level of confidence, you can easily become indestructible. Sometimes, others see confidence as a negative quality. We often call people with high levels of confidence self-centred, or "cocky." Perhaps some feel jealous or threatened by someone else's confidence, but you can't let this scare you away from being your best self. Once you achieve high self-esteem and higher confidence, you'll feel as though nothing can break your spirit. Sticks and stones may break your bones, but words will never hurt, right?

We've been told for so long and so often to not let what others say or do bring you down. We can all agree that's way easier said than done. Let's face it: it hurts when someone says or does something mean. Even if they weren't intentionally trying to hurt us, all too often we feel bad about ourselves because of something someone else might have said or done.

It's also important to constantly challenge your thoughts. When you look in the mirror and think, "why does my face look like that?" ask yourself immediately after where you originally heard those thoughts. Did someone used to make fun of you as a child? Maybe a parent or a sibling was a little too hard on you as you grew up? Sometimes, our negative thoughts don't come from anywhere else other than our own minds. Next time you say something mean to yourself, ask afterwards, where did I get that idea? Not everything you say to yourself is true! You can have all the tools necessary to make yourself feel better, and sometimes, nothing seems to work. We're going to discuss some ideas and tips to try and help you gain the most confidence possible.

You Don't *Need* A Partner

Before entering a relationship with anyone, you have to realize that you're doing so as a way to improve your life, not complete it. You should have the capabilities to go through your day to day life on your own, without needing anyone else's help. Yes, it's way easier to do simple things when you have a partner, but you need to remind yourself you don't *need* one. It's way easier to prepare dinner, pay for things, and especially raise children with someone else. A partner can take half the work load. That doesn't mean you can't do it alone. You're a strong independent woman that doesn't need a man to survive! You have to get to a point where you want one. Instead of something you need, they become someone you want to have around. Not only can that improve your relationship, but it can change your perspective on a lot more than just your romantic life.

A partner is a lot like milk with cereal. Cereal is great on its own, just snacking on the small pieces. But once you add the milk, it gets a whole lot better. Understand that you're still a valuable person without a partner. You don't need a man, you *want* one. Once you start accepting that truth, you'll realize different qualities in a partner that you didn't know you wanted. A romantic partner should be one that compliments you, not completes you. The thought of finding someone that you love so much you can't live without is a romantic and grandiose idea. It's not realistic, however. That kind of love can be painful and dangerous.

This also allows you to leave an unhealthy relationship should you find yourself in one. You should never find yourself in a position with a partner that you don't want to be with, only because you're scared that you might not make it without them. There have been plenty of stories of women staying with partners they didn't love only because they offered financial support. There are just as many cases of women dating men only because they're wealthy. Having financial support is amazing, but not as much as true love. Them having money should be a benefit, not a necessity.

The only person you should be depending on is you. You'll go through life much easier if you accept that you're the only one in charge of your happiness. Only you can control how you feel about certain things. It can be painful to wait for someone else to fulfil you or provide you with happiness. You have to learn to be the main provider of your own happiness and use the dating world as a way to have fun and improve certain aspects of your life.

If you look to another person to complete you, you can easily start to lose yourself. How many people do you know that become the person they're dating? Maybe they start liking a certain band or participating in hobbies they wouldn't normally. This is because they use dating as a way to fill part of their life. It's great to be dedicated to someone you love, and to enjoy the same things as them. However, when you let the person you're dating become your identity, you'll eventually have little of yourself left when it's all over.

Your Self-Esteem Has to Improve

One of the most challenging things you might face is learning to love yourself. In our capitalist society, we've been fed lies in order to buy into certain ideas. You're told you're overweight, so then you buy products and services to try and reduce your weight. Women are told their skin is too wrinkled as they age, so millions of dollars are spent a year trying to reduce the appearance of your age. There's nothing wrong with wanting to look your best, but some people take it to the extreme. Since women are told their whole lives how bad they look, of course, those thoughts have seeped into our every day mind. It can be hard to look into a mirror and not be critical of many things you see. It's a challenge, but one you can certainly overcome.

Others can see when you're feeling shy or anxious. You've probably noticed some nervous ticks on others before. Maybe they pick at their fingers or scratch their head. Others can notice this behaviour on you if you show any signs of anxiety. Not only is this distracting, but you also give those around you the notion that what you have to say might not be worth anything. If you don't even believe in yourself, how do you expect others to? We all have moments when we're nervous, but there's nothing more attractive than being secure with yourself. It lets everyone else know that you think you're great, which means you're probably great!

If you don't believe what you have to say, and offer is important, why should anyone else? The type of people who captivate their audiences are those filled with confidence. How many times have you seen an unattractive celebrity and wondered how they got to be so popular? There are plenty of famous people that aren't conventionally attractive, but still wildly successful. This is because they're filled with confidence. They believe in themselves and know that they have something to prove. People respond to this kind of confidence, and anyone is capable of having that power. You just have to navigate your anxieties and insecurities, constantly challenging your thoughts.

Humility cannot be forgotten, so it's about balance. No one likes the guy that thinks he's so great he can do no wrong. You still have to remain humble through your confident streaks, knowing that we're all inherently flawed. People that think their poo doesn't smell, for lack of better terms, seem unrealistic, so there's a lack of relatability. We all love someone that knows their worth, but still knows there's always room for improvement.

It's not easy. You're going to have days when you still hate what you see. You might wake up the next morning after a date and go over and over in your head about everything that you said that was wrong. You'll obsess over pictures that you took or that someone took of you, picking out every little detail that makes you look bad. This is because we've been trained to think this way. It's a habit that was forced into us as we grew up, so unfortunately, those thoughts will always be there. The older you get, the less you'll care, but in the meantime, you can practice building yourself up instead of breaking yourself down.

They'll Be Just as Scared as You

When facing a scary bug, like a spider, your mom might have told you not to be afraid. The spider is just as scared of you as you are of it! This is true about the people you're going to go on dates with. Dating is hard, and that's a pretty common idea. We're not saying anything new by bringing up the insecurities that can flood your brain during a date. Just remember this and know that you're not alone! The person across from you is just as anxious as you are. Maybe a little less, but maybe a little more, too. Don't be afraid to admit that you're nervous either! You don't want to be a blubbery mess, but sometimes just laying it out there can help calm you down. They might share they're nervous too, and the date will likely end up being a lot more relaxing.

Most people are more concerned with what they're doing and saying than what you are. In the moments that you're talking, they're listening, but they're also probably talking to themselves a bit, prepared for what they're going to say next. Maybe that day they spilled something on the shirt they wanted to wear, so now they're uncomfortable in a shirt that's too tight. Perhaps they're not as cute as their picture and they realized you were twice as good looking as they had originally thought. We all have experiences that make us nervous or anxious, so it can be easily assumed that others feel just as scared as you!

They probably won't pick up on the little things. They're just getting to know you. If this is a first date, that means you just met. They don't know your every little move or have predictions about the things you'll do and say. You do! You're with yourself every hour of the day, so you have a better grasp on the things you're doing. You can't expect the person you just met to know as much about you as you do about you. Make sense?

Are you more critical of yourself or others? Some people are way more judgmental of themselves than they are of others. You might think something that you do is stupid, but if someone else does the same thing, maybe you wouldn't think twice about it. Just try and practice treating yourself the way you would a friend. Before you take what you say to heart, would you say the same negative thing to your mom? Your sister?

All those moments of nerves ticking and stomachs turning, they're probably having too. When you're feeling nervous, choked up, or not yourself on a date, just remember that they might be feeling the same way! If they're not, and if they're someone that's way too confident, lacking total humility, you might consider that they wouldn't be someone you wanted to date anyway.

The Importance of Self-Care

An important step on the path to loving yourself is self-care. You've probably heard that word a lot lately. Some people use it as an excuse to take a bubble bath every day, or overeat fast food, but are they that wrong to do so after all? Our time on this planet is so short that we should spend as often as possible feeling good about ourselves! Bubble baths, treating yourself to takeout, and exotic facemasks are a key part in self-care, but know that it also goes deeper than that.

It's not just about doing your hair and wearing makeup. You give so much of your time every day to other people. Wherever you work, there's a good chance that you give someone you barely like 20-40 hours a week of your time. Perhaps you have a family member to take care of and a child yourself. It's important that in all the things you do, you make sure to set aside time for yourself. You don't want to lose who you are. Some think it's selfish to spend so much time alone, but it's important in maintaining who you are. It can be easy for your identity to fade when you give every moment of your life to other people. If you start to love yourself, it'll show! Not everyone has that open of a schedule but be sure to set aside a time at least once a week that you can treat yourself. It doesn't have to be a vacation or day at the spa, but you still need to remember to take care of yourself.

Take yourself on a date! As you navigate through the dating world, you're probably going to spend some money on someone else at a certain point. Why not take yourself on a date instead of someone else? This doesn't mean going to the store to pick up cat litter and getting fast food on the way home. Do something for yourself that you would do for the person you love. Go to a store, and even if you don't have money, take time to look at the things you like. Go see a movie alone and grab a nice dinner after. Pick a movie on TV and do a facemask while you indulge in a big meal. It doesn't have to empty your wallet, but it should be something just a little more special than your every day routine.

It all starts in your mind. Treat yourself the way you would treat the person you love the most. Like we said already, don't say anything to yourself you wouldn't say to a loved one. You're around yourself all day every day. Shouldn't you like that person? Shouldn't you want to treat them to something nice? Why not? This also means taking care of yourself on all levels. Eat healthy not because you want to crash diet, but because you want to feel good inside. Have a special skincare routine not because you want to look younger, but because you want your skin to be soft. Workout not so you can get a body that attracts others, but so it's easier to walk up the stairs and carry groceries from your car to the house. It might seem silly, or even feel selfish at times, but you have to do things for yourself.

Even on your bad days, take an extra step to give yourself some love. The most important thing to do on these bad days is remind yourself that it's OK! If you miss a day at the gym, don't break yourself down and feel guilty over not going. Remember that we all need to take a sick day every once in a while, even if we're not sick. You don't want to get into any bad habits, but that's because you just want what's best for yourself.

If They Leave, Let Them

All of what we discovered in this chapter is important, because if there comes a time that the other person leaves, you have to be strong enough to let them. That can be a big fear in a relationship. Wondering if they're going to leave you can be sickening, especially at the beginning of the relationship. You get used to having them around, wanting them to be there always. It's important to have a high level of confidence so that you know if they do leave, you'll be just fine. It's never easy to watch someone you love walk away, but if they don't love you, you have to let them leave.

If someone doesn't see your worth, that's on them. Once you've spent some time taking care of yourself and realized the amazing person you are, you'll also see that if someone wants to walk away from that, it's their loss. You won't be asking yourself, "what's wrong with me," and instead, "what's wrong with them?" Know that not everyone is meant for each other, and that sometimes, you're going to experience some heartbreak. That doesn't mean you're a bad person, or unlovable. It just means that you haven't hit the moment in the story that you meet your Prince Charming.

If they don't want you, you have to let them go. How many people do you know that tried to desperately get back together with someone that didn't want them in the first place? You will find someone that sees you and knows that they want to be with you. There won't be any guessing games, or moments wondering if they'll change their mind about you. Don't wait around for anyone, because there's always going to be someone waiting for you. It might not happen overnight, but it will happen, so you can't spend anymore time on someone that doesn't want you. The hardest part of letting someone leave that you loved is accepting that you weren't the right one for them. It can be hard to handle but know it doesn't mean anything bad about you. You probably have some friends that you adore, but you wouldn't date them, right? If someone doesn't want to be romantically involved with you, that in no way means you're a bad person.

Sometimes, you're mourning more than just the loss of a person. Maybe you were with someone for years, and then things ended. You probably thought about marriage, kids, and buying a house together. Perhaps you have your entire future mapped out with the person you have to watch walk out the door. Realize that you will find a new future. It can be scary to try and see your future in a different light. If a relationship ends, your next thought will probably be one of fear, wondering if you'll find anyone at all ever again. This is natural, but it doesn't mean that it's true. There will be someone out there, someone that loves you more than the person that decided to leave. Even if you never meet this person, wouldn't it be better to live a life happily alone than trapped in a loveless relationship?

There's always a worry at the end of a relationship that you might have wasted time. It can be hard to give up on something that you've invested time, emotions, and even money into. All the vacations, all the times spent with each other's families can feel like wasted moments if you decide to just end the relationship. You have to get this idea out of your head, however. Every moment you've lived has been important in defining who you are. It's good to have invested time in different relationships, as when you find the one that's right, you'll have all the knowledge from the past to improve your future.

Chapter 3: Finding the Right Partner

Finding someone single who wants to be in a relationship isn't always the hard part. Depending on your location that can certainly be a problem, but realistically, in any 25-mile radius, there's going to be a healthy handful of people that are single. The hard part, however, is that a lot of these people aren't going to be good matches for you. You might end up dating more than you have to in order to realize that, so we want to help make sure you're doing the best to find the partner that will compliment your life perfectly.

Decide What's Right For YOU

What do you want in a relationship? It's easy to look at a partner and know what you want. Someone handsome, with muscles, and the right haircut. That can be great for a fun night, but what do you actually want for your life? Go ahead and make a list of what things you want out of a relationship, not just a partner. Here are some ideas to get you started in case you aren't even sure what you want yourself:

1. A relationship with a lot of laughter.
2. A partnership in which they care for you as much as you care for them.
3. Unbreakable honesty and trust.
4. Constant support and appreciation.
5. The ability to be unapologetically yourself.

These are all things that might not be in every person you find, no matter how ideal they might be. Maybe you want to date a tall dark and handsome doctor with a great house. You could find him tomorrow, but is he going to have all the things on your list of what you actually want from a relationship?

Other people will try to tell you what kind of person to date. Maybe your parents have an idea of the kind of man they want you to end up with. Perhaps you come from a family of politicians, and they want you to marry someone with a notable political science degree. Maybe your mom doesn't want you to date anyone in the music industry, as she had her own heart broken by too many drummers. No matter who other people want you to date, you have to find a person that YOU want to date. It can be hard to tell if you're attracted to someone because they're good for you, or if it's because you *think* they're good for you.

The right person is different for everyone. Maybe you have sisters that all married lawyers. It'd be nice if you did too, but you absolutely loathe lawyers. You can't feel guilty about not being with someone that other people think is right for you. It's hard to not compare yourself to others, but just remember that Mr. Right can easily be Mr. Wrong for a different person.

Opposites attract, but sometimes dating yourself can work too. You probably know a couple of different romantic partners that seem like complete opposites. Then you might know someone that seems as if they're dating their clone. There's no strict rule to the type of person you should date. You have to define that yourself. If you're strong-willed and stubborn, an opposite might be better. If you're more relaxed and easy-going, a partner that's similar would be ideal. Everyone is different, so you have to accept that everyone's perfect guy is different as well.

At the end of the day, this is going to be a person you're sharing a bed with every night. You might find someone that seems to fill every quality on your mom's checklist. Everyone has a natural desire to please their parents, so maybe you go ahead on a few dates with this person in the hopes that they'll be the perfect one to bring home to your parents. You have to learn to accept that if they're not right for *you*, you have to let them go.

Know What to Look For

When it comes to online dating especially, people will list all sorts of qualities in their biographies. Just because they say they're one kind of person doesn't mean that's true. Everyone thinks that they're the easy-going, fun-loving person of their group. In reality, a lot of people can be pretty unaware of just how uptight or stressed they might be. Take all the qualities you see listed online with a grain of salt. At the same time, it's a good indicator if they have certain qualities listed in their biographies, because at least they desire to be the person they're describing in their biography.

What are the qualities you admire in the friends and family you keep close? This is another good list you could jot down. You have these people close to you for a reason, and if you explore that, it could help when you're looking for a romantic partner. Sometimes, you might not even realize what you're looking for until you look at the people around you. If you're a bold and talkative person, you might assume you want the same. Then you might look at your friends and realize most are a bit more relaxed and quieter. Maybe this is because your bold personality clashes with others. It's important to notice these behaviours so you don't end up picking someone that's completely wrong for you.

Honesty and trust are the greatest qualities. If they're willing to lie about something small, you never know how big of a fib they could be telling. If you end up meeting someone you met online, and they're shorter than they said, consider why they decided to lie. They might have just been insecure with their size and didn't want to get turned down because they're too short. There are other lies that can be concerning, however. If they're going to lie in the beginning, they're going to lie later on as well.

It's important to consider the things you like and dislike when finding a partner. Of course, it seems ideal to find someone that enjoys the same type of music and movies you do. However, you can't depend on this alone to find you the right partner. Having different taste is inevitable. Sometimes, having opposite opinions can add interest in a relationship, especially if you both enjoy critical discussion. Sometimes, others might have not experienced the same things as you, but if you start sharing music and interests, you'll discover you both have similar taste after all. When looking for love online, or even in the real world, it's important to not filter out those that don't love all the same things you do. A true relationship is strong beyond just the things that you both like.

At the end of the day, it's important to trust your gut when looking for the right person. There's a reason you're having that feeling! It's important to experiment with different dates that are opposite of you, but don't force yourself into anything you don't want. If someone is obviously going to be offended or dismissive of the things you like, it's completely fine to not give them a chance. Keep yourself open, however, and always be willing to try new things.

Warning Signs and Other Things to Avoid

How they treat other people is a direct indication of how they're going to treat you. If you go on a date and they're rude to the staff at the bar or restaurant you're in, they likely have little compassion for other people. If they don't seem to have a lot of friends, it might be because no one wants to be their friend. Not everyone has a huge social circle, and that's not a bad thing. You can still tell the difference between someone that doesn't have friends because they're a shy introvert, and someone who's alone because they're a jerk.

Some people think that controlling or jealous men can be a turn on. Unfortunately, there are a lot of women that think it's attractive when their men fight over them. This is just toxic behaviour and a sign that your man sees you not as a person, but as his property. A little jealousy is fine and to be expected. You'd likely be jealous of other women as well, but only to a certain point. If they become aggressive towards another man, or more importantly you, when faced with jealousy, it's best to just run from him ASAP. Being a little protective and jealous is a sign that they at least care about you, but too much proves that they have other tendencies that aren't healthy.

If a guy tells you that you're not like other girls, that's a sign he might be toxic. He's initially grouping all women into one group, seeing them as their stereotypes instead of individual people. If he says you're not like other people, that might be a little nicer rather than grouping you in with all the women in the world. He should see you as an individual person, not as a woman that he's set out to "conquer."

Another good question to ask in the beginning relationship is if they would do the same for you that you do for them. Maybe in the beginning you continue to go to his apartment, bars he likes, or order food that's his favourite. It's nice of you to be caring, but if he's not giving you the same consideration, you need to get out of there quick. If he can't put in the effort in the beginning of a relationship, you can bet it'll only get worse as things progress.

Here are some toxic qualities that could also become potentially dangerous. If you see any of these signs in your date, it's probably best to just avoid these people altogether and end things as soon as possible:
1. They describe one or more of their exes as "crazy"
2. They say something mean but mask it as them "joking"
3. They exhibit any sort of violence on the first or second date
4. They don't tip their bartender
5. They don't want to show any public affection or indication you're dating each other
6. They laugh at any of your dreams or goals
7. You find yourself afraid to share basic information with them
8. They monitor who you hang out with

9. They demand getting texted/called more frequently than you can handle
10. they don't know how to apologize or admit they're wrong

Small Things That Could Lead to Bigger Issues

Some of these might seem like forgivable qualities. Maybe you know someone already that has them, or you've experienced some of the list yourself. We've all made mistakes, but it's important to recognize these early on in a relationship because they could certainly only get worse. When it comes to physical violence or emotional abuse, it's important to leave the relationship as soon as something like this is detected. Abusers can be very manipulative and controlling, so you have to get yourself out before it's too late. Don't ignore the warning signs just because you really feel like you're falling for someone. That's how many people end up trapped in relationships they knew wasn't right in the beginning. It feels so good to start falling in love with someone and it can be easy to forgive the small things you don't like. As time goes on and the relationship progresses, that forgiveness will start to fade, and you'll be left having to confront the problems you spent so much time ignoring.

It can be challenging to look for signs in the blissful stages. When you're falling for someone, you have goggles that only allow you to see this person as a godly figure. They might do something wrong and you think to yourself that it's OK because they do this or that or have other qualities you admire. It can be scary to trust your gut as well but stay true to yourself and do your best to weed out the ugly. If your gut is telling you something isn't right, listen to that, don't pretend you didn't hear.

Think of a new relationship as if you're on vacation. You are having an absolutely amazing time, every step of the way. Maybe you're in a tropical destination or a cool city. You wake up happy, spend every moment having fun, and go to bed excited for more. On every vacation, most of us have an urge to live there! Who hasn't fantasized about just staying on vacation forever? You have to ask yourself, however, if you could actually live where you're vacationing. Could you handle the climate? The lifestyle? It's great at first, but if you actually lived there, it might not be the glamorous trip you imagined. The same can be said for a relationship. The beginning is always great, exploring every part of a new person. However, once that phase passes, is there still going to be something there that you can base a relationship on?

Some love stories seem so unachievable, but mostly because they are! When watching reality TV shows, or romantic movies, you might wonder why you can't have a relationship like that. They seem so in love, and it makes you wonder if what you have with your partner is real. That's because on TV, they don't live real life. They don't go grocery shopping together or share the moments in bed when someone is hogging the covers or snoring too loud. You're not going to find a flawless relationship, so don't compare yours to what you're seeing on TV.

It's OK to fight. Sometimes, it's actually better than not fighting at all. Fighting with someone allows you to think critically with them. It gives you a chance to honestly express your feelings and them the opportunity to do the same. Fighting can ruin a relationship, but it can also make one stronger. Too much fighting or fighting that gets violent is a clear warning sign that the relationship probably isn't right for you.

Don't Be Too Strict with Your Checklist

We strongly encourage you to write a list of the qualities you want in a person. We want you to be writing the entire time that you're reading this, but this is important now, just like the previous list of what you want in a relationship. If you compare the two lists, you might find that you want a completely different person than you originally thought. Some qualities you might consider are the age, appearance, occupation, and location of the person that you want to date. It's good to write these out to help you learn more about yourself and the things you want.

However, you can't use your list of qualities as a strict tool. You're likely not going to find the ideal person you wrote about in your journal. Maybe they have 9/10 qualities, so cutting someone out because they don't meet all ten is a bit foolish. Of course, you shouldn't date someone that's obviously wrong for you, such as an occupation, religion, or general outlook you don't agree with. You should still be open to altering the checklist, understanding that some people might have more qualities you didn't even have listed.

You might find someone that's completely opposite of what you wrote down, so don't let your list block you from exploring that relationship. It can be scary at first, especially if they don't seem to have any of the qualities you originally wanted. There are going to be cases of people like this catching your interest. It's completely OK to explore these relationships.

Have a few core values that you stick to, but don't let it blind you too much when seeking a partner. It's OK to stay strict with some things, especially if you have a religion or occupation that narrows the selection of people. It can be fun to go on dates with people different then you but picture your future and be sure that these differences would still workout in your everyday life.

This isn't just about getting a boyfriend. You want a partner. You don't just want someone that you can have sex with and take good Instagram pictures. You need a guy that will be there for you when you need him, and a guy that loves you as much as you love him.

Chapter 4: Attracting Other People

Your friends and family remind you often, at least they should be, that they'd love and support you no matter what. Unfortunately, the same graces aren't given by potential partners when entering a relationship. People are quick to make judgments. You could have some small behaviour that reminds them of their mother, so forever, they'll classify you as that sort of figure. It's not always going to happen, but you can certainly run into some judgmental men in the dating world. It's certainly the worst part about dating, but it is inevitable.

Putting yourself out there as a single woman means that you're putting yourself in a position to be judged. Many believe that men judge women harder than women judge men, but that line is a lot blurrier than you'd imagine. Most of the time, it's women that judge other women the harshest, but again, that's because what we've been taught in our society. We're all afraid of being judged, because we know deep down that we're so much more than the assumptions people have for us. Sometimes, the fear of judgement holds us back and keeps us from living our dreams! In order to enter the dating world, you have to be attractive to others on some level. With the tools we've already discussed and what we're going to be talking about in the rest of the book, that shouldn't sound so scary to you!

Find Out What Your Best Self Is

Now is the time to write a list of the things that you admire about yourself. This might be one of the most challenging lists to write. If we asked you to jot down everything you want to change about yourself, it might be a lot easier. You could probably write a novel about all the mistakes you've made or embarrassing moments. Who hasn't lied awake at night going over a situation in their head repeatedly? Instead of participating in that toxic behaviour, it's time to look into your mind and pick out the things you like about yourself!

Go ahead and write things you wish to achieve and goals you have for yourself as well. Maybe you want to travel somewhere or write a book! Even if it seems unachievable, write it down. Sometimes speaking things into existence can work! You should have a long list and collection of your positive qualities, your dreams, and your future goals. When we spend so much time tearing ourselves down, it can be hard to find the things that make us who we are. There's a reason why the people in your life that love you do so much! Even if it doesn't seem like it, we all have someone out there that admires us, and there's a reason for that.

Remember to improve yourself because you want to, not because you're trying to keep a man around. That way, if the unfortunate time comes that they do leave, it won't hurt so bad. Finding your best self is a way that you can boost your confidence, another important step in navigating the dating world.

Don't put so much pressure on yourself. Be as forgiving to yourself as you would be to a young child. Don't make yourself feel bad because you might have said the wrong thing. Instead, figure out what you didn't like about what was said and figure out how to improve it for the next time. There's no point in wallowing in self-loathing. It's time to be productive with your thoughts in order to be the best version of yourself possible.

We all have different versions of ourselves, and you have to pick out which one you like the most. Don't be anyone you're not just to fit someone else's idea of who you should be. We have our work persona, the personality we put on for our family, and the wild side that some of our friends can bring out. Work on harmonizing the best parts of these personalities, and you'll discover who you truly are.

Avoid Complaining

When meeting new people, we can often connect easiest by the common hatreds we share. There's a lot of things we could list out that people generally hate. Waiting, war and crimes, paying bills, and annoying political figures. Sometimes, our hatreds can bring us together, so it can be easy to have long conversations with our dates about all the things we both loathe.

It can feel natural and become easy to spend an entire date hating on the same thing. You have to avoid this, however. No one likes spending their time with a complainer. As we've discussed, there are plenty of commonly shared hatreds. Complaining about the weather with a co-worker is a good way to make the day go by a bit faster, but at the end of the shift, do you really feel all that more connected to the person? It's easy to glide through a conversation ripping apart a shared hatred, but it doesn't help you learn anything about the other person.

You can find common traits based in the way you judge and criticize different things, but you don't want to base your relationship on this. You'll get to the negative parts later in the relationship. Right now, take the time to get to know each other. Learn about what makes them happy, not what makes them annoyed. You could also risk having yourself associated with the hatreds discussed on the date. Even though you might've spent that time expressing that you too dislike the same things your date does, it could sour the mood and put a negative twist on the night.

Venting feels great, but it's not the way to start something, especially a relationship you want to build. If you notice that you and your date have been complaining for more than just a couple minutes, try to change the subject and twist it into something positive. Don't be afraid to call out the conversation either, by saying something like, "Instead of us talking about how much we hated the newest Marvel movie, why don't you tell me about a movie you saw recently you liked?" This comment could be used in many different ways and will help let your date know that you're not someone who spends all their time complaining. At the same time, ou don't want that quality in a partner.

Be Nice to The People Around You

Going out to a restaurant for a date seems basic, but there are so many interactions throughout the date that can give you insight to what your partner might be like in the real world. When the hostess tells them that it'll be another 10 minutes before you get a seat, does he roll his eyes, or does he smile and wait patiently? When the server greets you, does he give them a chance to talk or does he cut them off right away and put in his order? It's important that you're making the same effort to be kind to the staff at wherever you decided to have your date. He'll notice your behaviours in this regard the same way that you will.

When you meet someone, it can be hard to not picture what they might be like around their friends and family. They're going to be wondering the same thing, so it can be nice to bring them up as you're talking throughout your date. You can tell them about a tradition you and your friends have, or about the last present you gave your mom for her birthday. These are small and interesting topics that won't take up the entire date, but he'll notice your comments and formulate opinions based on the things you mention. If you bring up a fight you had with your sister on the first date, he might assume right away that you have trouble maintaining relationships with your family members.

How you treat just the bartender alone can give your date huge insight to how you're going to be acting towards them throughout the rest of the relationships, and you should take that into consideration as well. When just ordering a drink, there can be a test of patience, friendliness, and compassion, all within a matter of seconds. Don't let these interactions slide by and take these as opportunities to show him what kind of partner you would be.

If you get to go to their home, or let them into yours, how you interact with pets can be another indicator. I think we can all agree that if his dog likes you, that's a pretty good sign! Go out of your way to show him that you're a kind and considerate person. He'll remember those positive moments and take note of any warning signs he might notice in your interactions.

Just as he'll be paying attention to your interactions, you should be taking mental notes as well!

Ask Questions and Listen to The Answers

A first date is going to be filled with you and the other person asking a ton of questions. You're two people that just met, and who knows if this is the person you're going to be having children with! It's perfectly normal to ask questions, and you should! Trying to get to know the other person means that you care, and they'll realize this. Asking questions is great, because it helps keep the conversation going without the pressure. If there's a moment of silence, don't be afraid to ask them anything, such as what their favourite song or movie might be. They'll be expecting questions like this, so it's not like it'd be a strange thing to do. Don't be afraid to ask unique or strange questions either, as it'll help keep the night interesting! Here are some unique questions you could ask your date when you're feeling uncomfortable:
1. What's the last thing you bought that you regret purchasing?
2. What's an embarrassing story your mom would tell me if I called her right now?
3. If you found out you had to move away tomorrow, where would you go?
4. What's the worst gift you've ever received?
5. What's the best prank you've ever pulled?

Don't turn it into a job interview. You should be having fun and getting to know your date, not grilling them to find out if they meet ever point on your checklist. Make sure that you're actually listening to what they say as well. They'll notice if you're just breezing through and trying to make it to the next question.

You're going to want to ask a lot, and it's completely fine if you write down a list of questions you want to ask before going on the date. Just don't take the list with you, of course. Figure out what else you might want to know about the person before going on the date. Did they share something funny on their dating profile that you need more explanation for? Maybe they shared very little information and you don't know much about them at all.

Listening to the answers is important. Instead of going through the list of things you want to ask, it's important to actually listen to the answers so you can form conversations from that. Maybe you only make it to the first question and the rest of the night is conversation after conversation that flows perfectly. Actually, engaging in a conversation is more important than anything else.

People love talking about themselves! Your date won't be mad if you make an effort to get to know them. Just remember, if they don't share the same curiosities that you do, they might not be right for you. If you notice that you've been doing all the question-asking, it could just be because they're nervous. It could also mean that they're more self-centred than you'd like.

Stay True to You

Remember, you're doing this for yourself! You might have a child already and you're looking for another parental figure for them. Even if that's the case, dating is still about finding the right person for you. You can't compromise who you are or any of the ideas you have just in an attempt to impress someone else. You could go into the date as a completely different person, and maybe they end up liking that fake person. Are you going to keep up the façade for the rest of your life? You have to be yourself, because that's the easiest. If they don't like who you are, they know where the door is.

You're going to have qualities that some people don't like. You could be voted the most beautiful woman in the world, but there's still going to be that one guy that just doesn't find you attractive one bit. Remember, that's his fault, not yours! Never, ever change anything about you to suit someone else. If they don't like who you are, tell them to go find someone they do like. There are even people that don't like pizza or chocolate, so you have to accept that some people just won't like you. Don't let this defeat you. Let it be a reminder that when you do find someone that adores you, it will be amazing.

When it comes to bad habits that you might have, like smoking, your partner might want you to change this. If they express ideas like this, it isn't always bad. You just have to look at what they're asking of you and why they might be doing so. Do they want you to quit smoking because they care about your health, or because they just don't think it's attractive? If someone wants to change your bad habits, that can be an indication that they actually care about you and your health. However, don't let someone convince you that a normal quality you exhibit is a bad habit. If you find yourself compromising who you are or what comes naturally because your date doesn't like that quality, it's a sign they might be too controlling.

It can be hard to be yourself, especially if you're still not even sure who that is. If you stay authentically you, you'll find your way. It's going to be hard, but it's going to be very worth it in the end.

There's no one out there worth compromising who you are for. For every person that you meet that doesn't like you, you'll find two that do! It can be hard to let go of someone that you might be falling for because they don't like you as much. You have to let them go, because if they don't love you for everything you are, they aren't the one.

Chapter 5: Navigating Online Dating

It can be crazy to think of how just a few decades ago, if you wanted to find a date, you might take out a classified ad in the newspaper. They didn't have computers in their pockets and every other technology capable of finding a partner. You might have even had to meet someone, like a dating or relationship expert, before landing a few dates. Nowadays, it seems as though the only way that people meet is online. If you ask couples how they've met, most will say either through work, school, or online. There aren't cute stories of how people met as often, which can be sad sometimes. On the other hand, how lucky are we that we could potentially find a soulmate with the touch of a button? You can select what kind of person you're looking for just as you might a new television you're buying online. That thought can terrify some, but excite others.

If you're not online, you might be a little behind in the dating world. Even if you do meet someone in person, there's a good chance they're already on different dating apps and websites. That's just the way the world works now, and whether you like it or not, it's gotten too big to fight. If you can't beat them, join them. If you're reading this book and you haven't gone online yet, that's your first step. It can be scary, but you'll be shocked to find out just how many people there are in the world that are trying to date you.

You're still going to meet people you might want to date in the real world, but in the society, we live in, it can still be important to get online and go on some dates. You don't have to give up hope that you might find Mr. Right in your favourite coffee shop after a chance encounter. You do have to accept that the world is changing, and the person that's meant for you might be making their Tinder profile right now. There are plenty of people that are resistant to the technological world that surrounds us, but so many have found love through online dating that it's clear we can't fight it any longer.

Tinder Secrets

There is an endless amount of dating sites that you could choose to use. There's even a website specifically for farmers that want to date other farmers. You can make profiles based on your religion, and some sites even help you find a sugar daddy. We have endless options when it comes to making dating profiles, but there are some clear winners that everyone seems to be using. Tinder is certainly a popular choice, and the style of the app is becoming common for other dating sites. Swiping right or left has really simplified the way we look at dating and potential partners. It can seem weird to be able to have this power in your fingertips, so we're going to offer some tips to help you navigate this crazy world.

Never lie on your profile. This is probably one of the most important rules. It can be tempting to crop out your body and use a slimming picture of your face. You might even want to lie about where you work or exaggerate how much time you spent in school. While this is certainly possible to do when making profiles online, you should avoid this at all costs. Lying online only sets you up for future failures. They're going to find out you look nothing like your picture or that you fibbed about how much money you might have. You want someone to fall in love with you, not with a complete stranger. Lying can become tricky in more ways than just getting confronted with the truth. Some people find themselves addicted to the thrill of lying, and end up using somebody else's picture completely, catfishing potential dates. This is not only harmful to the potential date, but you're hurting yourself in the process as well. Nothing good comes from lying, at least long term. It might feel good at first, but you're only going to get yourself in trouble.

Look at it as an outsider. If one of your friends is currently online dating as well, take the opportunity to look at your own page through each other's profiles. Take the chance to see what others see when they click on your profile. Put yourself in the shoes of your potential date, and ask yourself if you didn't know who you were, would you like what you saw? Would you swipe right or left on yourself? You might think you have the best profile you've seen, but when you really take a moment to step back and see your page from an outsider's perspective, you could see exactly what others are seeing.

Ignore people that might try to bug you. You're going to run into people that try to tease you, and maybe take things a little too far online. If it's some harmless joking, do your best to ignore these people. Maybe they'll make a comment about your profile picture, or something silly you had in your biography. If it seems like they're only trying to get a rise out of you, just ignore them. There are plenty of people on the internet that just want attention no matter if it's good or bad, so don't give them any. If someone is legitimately harassing or cyber bullying you, be sure to report them immediately. Even if you don't take personal offense to their harassment, there might be someone else out there that could get serious emotional trauma from an online interaction. Do your best to help weed out the ugly on the different dating apps you're using.

Remember, it's just an app. There are way too many people that can become dangerously addicted to their power to swipe right or left. At the end of it all, remember to not take things too seriously. The outcome of what's happening as you're navigating the online dating world could be very serious, especially if it results in a spouse and children. At the same time, it's an app that you might have stored next to your favourite game. You can't take something like that too seriously. Don't forget that you're supposed to be having fun in this process! If online dating isn't working for you, there are other options, but know that this is certainly the easiest.

Making A Good Profile

Don't go overboard when it comes to creating a dating profile. The more you build yourself up, the higher the expectations your date will have. If you go on and on about how amazingly perfect you are on your profile, your date is going to be expecting that same level of perfection. Don't sell yourself short, but there's certainly a fine line between building yourself up and creating a fake online personality. Don't use only vacation pictures if you don't actually enjoy travelling that often. Nothing bad will happen if you just remain true to who you are and make an honest profile that represents who you really are.

Keep it real. You don't want to seem unapproachable. If you do make a profile that makes you out to be some sort of superhero, you might find that you're not getting as many messages as expected. You could have the best-looking profile compared to everyone else, but fewer messages. You want to make sure that you still seem approachable and as a real person that anyone could date. There will be plenty of guys that would see your meticulously crafted profile and think you might be too good for them. They might fear that you already have too many male suitors and not even make any effort at all. Make sure that your online profile reflects a real person that isn't too scary to reach out to.

Avoid using selfies. Selfies are great. Who doesn't like taking pictures of themselves? When it comes to online dating, profiles that don't have selfies as their main picture end up doing better. Anyone could take a picture of themselves, but not everyone could go for a hike, or party at a cool brewery. Try to use pictures of you doing things as your main profile. If you just use another picture of your face, you'll be grouped in with the rest of the girls that just have pictures of their faces. Instead, use a photo of you in a cool setting, or holding a cute pet. Show people that you do something other than take pictures of yourself.

Always have an original biography. You might find a joke online that you think is funny, but so have ten other people in your area. Nothing is a bigger turnoff than being confronted with a person just like everyone else. If you use someone else's quote, joke, or rip off a biography entirely, you're letting potential suitors know that you don't have much originality. Make sure that you craft a completely authentic biography so as to really stand out. If you can't think of a funny joke, that's totally fine. The cheekiest biographies aren't always the ones that get the most messages. You can prove you're funny later.

Swipe right as often as possible. If you're not sure about a person, swipe right. If they seem perfect but look kind of funny in their picture, swipe to keep them. The worst that could happen is that you don't match. That doesn't mean you shouldn't try in the first place. Obviously, if they're doing something offensive in their picture or their biography, avoid them at all costs. Don't swipe someone away forever just because there was something small you didn't like about them. You might see something that turns you off, but there's always a chance that you're just misinterpreting something small. Give everyone a chance until they give you a bigger reason not to. Who knows if you've already swiped away your soulmate because you saw a poster on the wall in the background of their profile picture. Maybe they were just taking a picture at someone else's house! It's always worth it to just give everyone a shot, even those you would least expect to be attracted to.

Meeting Online People IRL

Never meet anyone at their home. This goes without saying, but for real, make sure that your first meeting with an online date is in public. No one that ends up in a sketchy situation ever thinks that they're going to be the one to wind up there. It might seem lame to be cautious, but it's even lamer to wind up dead or hurt when you didn't have to. As a woman, you have to be especially careful before meeting up with someone. Make sure you discuss the bar or restaurant you're going to and do your research before you go. Be sure it's in an area that has plenty of other activity happening around as well to avoid going to the middle of nowhere. Figure out a plan should you have to leave early. Is there public transportation or a safe spot to park your car? Could you take a cab or Uber should you have to? You might end up really liking the person and wanting to go home with them right away but be sure to be extremely safe about every decision you make when meeting an online friend in person.

Tell at least two people where you're going to be. You might not want to share that you're dating with certain people. Friends might get too nosy, and your parents might get too excited. You don't always have to tell people you're going on a date. Just mention you're meeting a friend for the first time and you want to make sure you have backup should you need it. We're not telling you this to scare you. There's a good chance you could go on fifty dates and never once run into danger. There's also a chance that the first and only date you go on could be one that turns bad quick. You never think it's going to happen to you. You never assume that you're going to be put into a potentially dangerous situation, but it can happen. You shouldn't fear or expect it, but just be prepared should it happen.

Don't have expectations too high. Picture this: you meet the perfect guy online, or so you think. You spend a week or so chatting with them online, eventually getting their number. He asks you on a date and you agree, blissfully telling your friends and family that he's the one. Everything you saw online about him was perfect, and his profile pictures are to die for. Once you finally meet him, however, you realize he has a strange voice and his teeth are a little more crooked than in the pictures. It's going to happen. You're going to meet people that are different than your perceptions, and you have to be ready for that. Our brains do a good job of filling in the blanks between the pictures and information we've gathered about a person online. They don't always create the right picture, however. Don't have expectations for a person set so high that when you meet them, you get disappointed. There are going to be things about them that you guessed exactly right, but there are also going to be some differences you weren't expecting.

Be honest at the end of the night. If you had a terrible date and hope to never see that person again, you don't have to say those exact words, but let them know that'll be the last date. You can think of something to soften the blow, or just tell them straight up you don't think you're right for each other. Save the other person the agony of wondering how things went at the end of the date. Maybe they'll even be able to convince you to go on a second date, even though you were already planning on ghosting them halfway through the dinner. Also, be sure to be honest if you know that you really liked the person. Tell them honestly that you hope to see them again. You can gauge their reaction to see if they feel the same way instead of staying up all night for the next three days, wondering desperately when they're going to text you. Honesty up front only means that you're setting a precedent for honesty later.

Don't delete your profile right away. So, you finally go on a date that really makes you feel something. There's an undeniable gut feeling that HE IS THE ONE. Before you go picking out wedding dresses and deleting all your online dating profiles, give yourself a little reality check. You're going to have a lot of good first dates. You'll have a lot fewer good second dates, and even fewer good third dates. It's going to seem great at first, but don't let yourself get too caught up in a fantasy. It can be easy to build something up only to watch it desperately crumble right after.

There's No Rush

If you meet someone you really like, you might start to feel the pressure to talk to them immediately, set up another date ASAP, and, like we've previously discussed, delete your online dating profiles. You can't rush into things, however, as you still need to be careful. You might feel the pressure that they could be going on other dates when you're not together. You might worry yourself by thinking that he's going to swipe right on another girl right after he does you. If it's the real deal, it's going to find a way. Don't put pressure on the relationship right away, or else you're going to set yourself up for heartbreak.

The person that you might be falling for isn't going to leave you overnight. If he does, well good riddance. If he didn't feel as strongly for you as you did for him on the first date, then it's probably for the better that he decided to move onto someone else. Don't put so much pressure on the relationship right in the beginning. You can't expect him to have the same feelings right away. Some people take more time than others to realize what they want and what they have.

If you put too much pressure on something, it's going to break. Don't force yourself into something you're not sure about just because you're feeling the pressure.

Go at your own pace. Never let anyone force you into an uncomfortable situation. Just as we're warning you to take things slow, make sure your dates offer that same luxury for you. Don't let someone make you feel as though you owe them anything. If someone's pressuring you into a relationship you're not ready for, don't submit just out of fear or guilt. You have to trust your gut, and the right person would never make you do anything you didn't want to. You want to date someone with patience and understanding, so if they're forcing you to agree to a relationship you're not ready for, they're clearly lacking both of those qualities.

Be Safe with An Open Mind

Your safety is the most important thing at the end of the day. Interacting with other humans can always be potentially dangerous, but you can't live your life in fear. You do, however, have to live your life as prepared as possible. You never want to get blindsided by a potentially harmful situation. People can be very manipulative and controlling. You might not realize you were tricked until it's too late. Not only can people be potentially violent, they can also be con artists that use you for money. Never give anyone money online, but that should also go without saying. There are plenty of people that form relationships with others online just so they can get some bills paid or extra spending money. If someone asks you for money before you meet, there's a good chance that's all they're after. You have to protect yourself in more ways than one.

Online dating is pretty strange. You can find yourself in an odd situation that might seem unexplainable. You put pictures of yourself online, let others decide if they want to date you, and then you meet them, sometimes in a place you've never been before. We do some strange things for love, but it's clear that it's worth it in the end. If love was meaningless and finding a partner wasn't important, people wouldn't be spending all this time and money on dating.

You still have to have an open mind. You're going to have some random encounters and it's not always going to be easy. The prize at the end is so amazing, however, that putting up with everyone can be worth it all.

Don't be afraid to send the first message! Sometimes, for women especially, it can be scary to send the first message. You might be afraid that it seems too desperate or needy to be the one reaching out. There are plenty of guys that like when a girl makes the first move! Who knows if a guy is too shy to reach out as well. You never want to miss out on something potentially amazing just because you're afraid of what could happen. The worst thing you could experience is not getting a message back!

Chapter 6: Some Dating Tips You'll Actually Use

You can google dating tips, ask your friends for advice, or buy countless books on dating. There might be some helpful information, but a lot of tips are unrealistic, or give you advice in areas that aren't really needed. We have some legitimate tips for you that will actually work.

Keep in mind, that everyone is different. There aren't any exact rules of how to do things, so don't put too much pressure on yourself. We've said that a lot in this book, but it's incredibly true. You can't be too hard on yourself during a process that's already challenging enough. Even though everyone is different, these are some dating tips that will help everyone.

Getting Ready Before

Don't decide what to wear until the day of. You might have the urge to go out and buy a new outfit for your date but try to resist. Some new shoes or a cute dress might help, but don't rely fully on a brand-new outfit for your date night. Instead, wait until you wake up the day of the date to see how you're feeling. Each day is different, and you never want to assume what your mood might be. You might wake up wanting to wear something plain and simple, or perhaps it's a day to be adventurous. Wait until you see how you're feeling on the day of the date to make sure that you're as comfortable in what you're wearing as possible.

Now's not the time to experiment with your hair and makeup. Maybe you've always wanted to wear red lipstick but were never brave enough. There's a time and place to experiment with your hair and makeup, and the day of your first date is not that time, unfortunately. You don't want to make yourself anymore nervous or anxious than you already might be. If you try something new, you might end up focusing on that the entire date rather than any conversations you're having. You might try a new hairstyle, only to realize that the restaurant is humid, and it made your 'do completely fall apart. Just keep it simple and work with what you're used to. Experiment new looks with your friends and other people that are willing to be a little more honest!

It's perfectly fine if you want to have a drink or two. While you're getting ready is a great time to pour a glass of wine or mix a cocktail. Put on some music that makes you feel good about yourself and have fun getting ready. A drink could certainly relax you but remember to keep it limited. You don't want to show up already drunk! The same goes for when you're actually on the date. You'll probably be nervous to the point that you're going to want to do a round of shots. Make sure to not drink too much, as you might end up embarrassing yourself or doing something you regret. Being nervous is uncomfortable, but it's better than getting so drunk you don't even remember the date.

Make sure to spend some time alone during the day before the date. You don't want to forget yourself in this process. Have a moment alone, even if it's just twenty minutes, to just relax and zone out. Maybe take some time to look over all the lists we've had you write so far while reading this book. Be sure to check in with yourself and make sure that you're staying true to who you are.

Always Show Up

There are going to be some days that you just want to no call and no show your date. You might have had a bad day at work and all you want to do is go to bed when you get home. You might find yourself regretting scheduling the date. Maybe it's the only thing you have to do that day and the thought of going makes you so nervous that you want to cancel the occasion. Don't let yourself treat the date like a responsibility. No matter what you might be feeling before the date, just go! Force yourself to get out of bed or off the couch. You don't want to miss out on meeting Mr. Right because you were too lazy to take a shower!

Get ready for the date and actually show up to the bar. Maybe you're regretting the date because it's with someone that you just don't see yourself with. At least get ready for the date and start to head there before cancelling. This way you can see if the nerves about the date are because of who you're meeting or just because you didn't want to have to leave your home.

If you still feel like it's just not the right person for you, go ahead and cancel. There's no use in wasting each other's times. At this point, you should still be ready to go, so maybe you could head to a different bar and have a drink alone. This could be your chance to at least take yourself on a date. Never let yourself cancel on account of not wanting to go out. You're going to have lazy nights where you just want to stay in your pyjamas, but that's not how you're going to meet Mr. Right! Save those pyjama nights for when you're months into the relationship and you have someone next to you to binge your favourite TV shows. Now is the time to do things that scare you!

Be sure that you're cancelling because it's not right, not because you're just scared. Even if you have to cancel last minute, at least you can't say you didn't still try. If you're unsure about the person, still go on the date to make sure that you're giving them a chance. You might find that it's the best date of your life. You would never want to wonder if you cancelled on the person that you're supposed to end up with.

Make sure to tell them you're not going to make it and be honest. It can be awkward to have to cancel, but it's better than completely ghosting them. Getting stood up on a date can be pretty painful. If you leave someone to sit alone at a bar and wonder where you are, it could really kill their spirit. You don't want to make someone else feel as though there's something wrong with them.

Who Pays?

For decades, it's been assumed that the man is going to pay. This mostly stems from men being the providers and women being the ones to work from home. While that's still true for some people, the majority of women in the dating world have their own jobs now and can provide for themselves. We have to wonder now if this means that the days of expecting for the man to pay are over? Women still only make change on the dollar when it comes to the overall statistics of American gender economics. However, since it's 2018, it's time to question what it might mean if the woman decides to pay instead of the man.

It's up to you how to go about the date, and there are different meanings behind what you might choose. It's completely up to you and your date when it comes to deciding who is going to pay. There's no wrong way to do things, and whatever you're most comfortable with is completely fine. A good rule of thumb, in case you're not sure, is to let whoever did the inviting pay. So, if he asks you to go out for drinks, let him pay! If you decide to make the first move and schedule a date, you should be ready to pay for the both of you. He might still want to pay if you take him out, and vice versa. Let's talk about what that could mean to your date.

Letting him pay is completely fine. It doesn't mean you're a submissive woman, or not a true feminist. Some women fear that if they let a man pay, he'll be expecting something at the end of the night. This is complete bogus. You don't have to have sex with someone just because they paid for your drinks and meal. If he is someone that actually expects this, then don't give him any and let him leave. At least you'll get some free drinks in the process! If you want him to pay no matter what, a good trick is to go to the bathroom once you're expecting the bill to come. This way, he'll be left alone with the bill and he has to make the decision on his own.

Splitting the bill is another great way to set a precedent for the future. He might be the type of guy that needs to pay to feel better about himself, so you can let him if he must, but offering to split the bill at least lets him know where you both might stand in the relationship. It's a good way to show that you're in it just as much as he is. Don't force yourself into this situation if you can't afford it, however. If you went somewhere really nice and it's clear he has more money than you, offer to pay for the tip. It shows that you're concerned about what the waitstaff is getting, and that you're willing to help out a bit, but only as much as you can. If he's a lawyer and you're on a cashier's salary, it doesn't make sense to split the $200 bill. Paying the $40 tip could really show him that you're not there just for financial support.

If you decide to pay, that tells him right away what kind of woman he's going to be dating. You let him know from the first date that you're an independent woman and you won't be needing any of his financial assistance. For some men, this is a complete turn-on. How many dates do you think he's been on where the girl forced him to pay by slipping away to the bathroom once the bill came? Now he gets the chance to enjoy the night without having to pull out his credit card. Who knows, maybe you'll make him wonder if he has to give something up at the end of the night. Only joking of course. Be careful if you do decide to pay, as some men might think this is a turn-off. There are certain men that feel the need to provide. They might want to pay to fill some part of their ego. If you want to avoid this kind of man, paying is a good idea in order to scare them away.

Don't Do Anything You Don't Want

Let's not beat around the bush, sex is a big part of what both people are seeking when they go on a date. If you're seeking out someone to become your life partner, you have more on your mind when meeting them than if they're good in bed. You can't deny that the thought pops into your head a few times throughout the date. You two won't talk about it until it comes to the end of the night, but the thoughts will still be there. Just make sure that you don't go into the date with any expectations or pressures. You might want to prepare yourself in case it does happen by doing some extra grooming or stashing some overnight clothes in your bag, but never assume that you're going to be having sex on the first date. You can't make a decision for yourself, for your body, before you meet the person.

There's no written rule anywhere that says you have to sleep with someone on the first date. There's also no rule that says you can't go ahead and jump into bed with them right away. We hear all sorts of pressures and rumours about what the unspoken rules of dating are. Just know that there is absolutely no rule, law, or any sort of demand anywhere that says you have to do a certain thing on the first date. It is your body, so you decide what happens with it at the end of the night. Remember that this is true from the moment you go on the date to wherever you end up that night. If you agree to go back to his apartment after the date for more drinks this DOES NOT mean that you have consented to anything sexual. Don't ever let him make you feel this way. Even if he bluntly asks if you want to have sex and you say yes, you can change your mind at any time.

The most important decision you can make on that night is one that makes you the most comfortable. It doesn't matter if it's the sixth date and you two are already laying naked in bed with each other. If you don't want to have sex, DON'T. Someone that actually cares about you would never force you into an uncomfortable situation. Also, don't let him try and convince you that "blue balls" is a real thing. Even if it were, offer up a bag of ice, not your body for him to use. He'll survive, and if he doesn't, then that's on him. It's not your fault because you didn't want to have sex with him.

If he gets upset that you don't want to have sex, let him be mad. If he threatens to leave, or to go find someone else that will have sex with him, LET HIM LEAVE. Even if it's someone you've already invested a lot of time and money into, you can't be forced to do something you don't want to. You don't want to have to give any of yourself or your time to a man that just wants to use you. Make sure that he knows that no means no. Don't let him berate you and ask you over and over again to have sex until you're so beaten down that you just say yes to get it over with. This is not OK. It might seem obvious when reading this, but many women don't realize they're in a dangerous situation until after the fact. It can be hard to recognize what's going on at the time, but if you feel uncomfortable at all, just leave. If he's worth keeping around, he'll understand.

If he thinks you're any kind of woman because you had sex, let him leave now too. You might have the anxiety that if you sleep with him on the first date, he'll form his own opinion on you. If you want to have sex with him and he wants it too, go for it! You're both consenting adults and you should be having fun. If you're worried that he's going to judge you, think you're easy, or not want to have a committed relationship with you, don't stress. If that is who he really is, then you don't want him anyway. You don't want to date someone that thinks a woman is any less just because she's had more sexual partners. A man that really loves and cares about you would do so whether you've slept with 1 man or 100 men.

It's Supposed to Be Fun

The only way to online date wrong is when you're not having fun! We've discussed a ton of different tips, tricks, and secrets up until this point. Remember that none of them are rules, regulations, or some sort of unwritten law. These are all just suggestions and tips to help make sure you're having as much success and fun as possible. You don't have to listen to what we're saying, just listen to your gut! It's all about you at the end of the day and finding something that improves your life. It's going to be stressful at times, and you might even end up hurting at one point. The overall idea is still to just have fun, so if you're not doing that, you might want to reevaluate why you're doing this in the first place.

Take a break if you have to, there's no pressure. If you've gone on ten dates and you just don't have it in you to go on anymore, it's completely fine to take a break. It's not a race, so don't force yourself to keep going if you don't want to. Someone once said, "love is like a fart. If you have to force it, it's probably shit." It's a pretty lame saying, but it's true! Love isn't going to be easy all the time, but it shouldn't be that hard. Sometimes, when we're desperately looking for a partner is when we have the worst luck. When you're least expecting it, you might end up finding the love of your life.

Be honest with yourself before everything else. You might find someone that you really like, but on the fourth date, you're not feeling that romance anymore. Just because you've invested time into someone doesn't mean you have to stay. Getting hurt is no fun, but sometimes, having to hurt someone else is the hardest part. You have to be honest with yourself, and don't force yourself into a relationship you don't want just because you feel guilty. You don't owe anyone anything. Well, you do actually owe yourself something, and that's happiness. You deserve happiness and you deserve to be loved. Any situation that makes you feel like this is unachievable is not the right one for you.

Find someone that makes you laugh. In all the couples that you know that have seemingly lasted a lifetime, what's one thing they have in common? There's a good chance that they make each other laugh, a lot. You should find someone that does the same thing for you. You don't have to go out and find your local stand-up comedian but look for someone that you can joke with. Find a person that understands your sense of humour, not one that makes you feel bad about the dirty jokes you might make. You could find someone that has a mansion, and endless amount of money, the body of a pro-athlete, and the face of a Greek god, but if they don't make you laugh, are you really going to find happiness with them?

You're allowed to just be friends. Sometimes it can be hard to end a relationship because you genuinely enjoy hanging out with that other person. Just know that becoming friends is an option! Be honest with them and say that the romance isn't there but that you just want to spend time with them. It might be weird at first, but only if you let it become awkward! Don't stay in a romantic relationship you don't want just because you don't want to let that person go. If there's a connection there, you two will find a way to be friends.

Chapter 7: Maintaining the Relationship You Worked For

You did it! You found someone you actually want to be around, and they like you back! It was probably a lot of work, some compromise, and an endless number of butterflies in your stomach. Just know that not everyone will find this in their lifetime. Some people will go forever without meeting someone they like. Others might end up stuck in a relationship that never completely fulfills them. You made it to this point, and we're going to let you know how to best keep up your newfound romance.

Dating was hard but maintaining this relationship can be just as challenging. There are going to be moments of questioning and days you just want to give up. Remember that living with yourself can be hard enough. You have moments where you're too hard on yourself, or days that you can't even get out of bed. You have to realize that those same feelings and doubts are going to pop in with the person that you're becoming closest with. There are going to be moments of doubt when you wonder if there's someone better out there. This is completely natural but it's no reason to end your relationship.

If you're in love, it shouldn't be that hard, but understand that no relationship is easy. There might be a time when you realize that the good parts no longer outweigh the bad anymore. It might be time to let go, but don't give in so easily. We're going to help you navigate through this relationship with the following tips.

Know Your Voice and Use It

The worst kind of partner you could find is someone that doesn't listen to you. Sometimes your emotions might be a little crazy and you might have days when you're acting a bit irrational. Your partner should still listen to your feelings and validate them as often as possible. You're never wrong for having the feelings that you do. What matters is how you handle those feelings. Your partner should be someone that you're willing to talk to and someone that you're not afraid to share your thoughts and fears with. Even if you're having doubts about the relationship, you should be able to go to your partner with these fears without being scared of how they'll react.

You might become more submissive as the relationship goes on. You've invested so much time, and now you don't want to lose them by doing or saying the wrong thing. Something that might have bugged you in the beginning you stay quiet about now just to keep the peace. It happens and it's completely normal to want to just stay quiet about something that makes you upset to avoid a fight. Know that when this does happen, you should still voice your opinion. You don't want to be forced into a corner in your relationship with no way to talk yourself out. Don't let your partner make you feel as though you have to put up with what they do just because you're afraid of losing them. That's not what a relationship should be.

A relationship is filled with compromise. Know that you're going to have moments that you have to sacrifice certain things for your partner. One of the worst parts of being in a relationship is having to share! You might want to eat the dessert all by yourself, but your boyfriend or husband might ask for a bite. Just wait until you have kids! In a good relationship, however, compromise should be easy. You should want to share with this person not because you have to, but because you want to. The sacrifices you make shouldn't cause you too much pain and turmoil because you know that you're doing so to make someone you love happy. If it gets to a point that you feel as though you're sacrificing too much, you might want to take a step back and look at the bigger picture. Is your partner being too selfish? Are they not compromising just as much as you?

Your relationship should be 50/50 and if it's not, it's time to question what it's all worth.

Don't let anyone make you feel as though what you're stating is wrong. We've set it before and we'll say it again: you're not wrong for feeling the way you do. How you handle those feelings is what's important. Let's look at this through an example. Your boyfriend tells you that he's going to a party and you know that one of his ex-girlfriends is going to be there. You can't go because you're working. The feeling you might have first is jealousy. THIS IS OK. You're allowed to be jealous, especially if he's going to be around someone he was once in a relationship with. What might not be OK, is how you choose to handle that feeling. If you decide to call in sick to work so you can secretly follow him to the party and watch every move he makes from a bush outside a window, well, that's kind of crazy. How you should handle it is by being honest with your partner and let him know you're feeling a little jealousy. If he makes you feel bad about being jealous, that's wrong. Instead, he should offer reassurance that you have nothing to worry about. What you feel is never wrong, it's just how you handle those feelings that could cause issues.

How he handles your feelings is important as swell. Gaslighting is a huge problem in relationships. Gaslighting is when someone makes you feel as though you're crazy for having the feelings that you do. Your partner might be gaslighting you if they manipulate your own feelings to trick you into thinking that your sanity is unstable. If he uses any of these phrases when confronting him about your feelings, he might be gaslighting you.
1. You're too sensitive
2. You're being crazy
3. I'm sorry that you feel that way
4. You're remembering things wrong
5. You always do this
6. Here we go...
7. You're making things up

8. You're getting too upset over this
9. What about what you did to me?
10. Can't you just let things go?

You're Going to Have to Compromise

Compromise is more than just watching a movie or eating at a restaurant that you don't really want to. It might be going to their hometown for Christmas since they haven't seen their mom in five years. Maybe it's not drinking around them because they're a recovering alcoholic. In order to enter in a relationship, you have to expect to be selfless at times, because they should be giving the same treatment back to you.

You have to make sure that they're giving just as much as you. When making a big decision that could seriously affect your life, always ask if they would do the same for you. Maybe they got a job in California and want you to move with them, but you have no friends or family on the west coast. This would be a huge lifestyle change, but for the right person, it could happen. Before you pack your bags, ask yourself if they would do the same thing for you? If the answer is no, you're likely compromising too much for your relationship.

Don't avoid fighting too much. Sometimes it can be easier to just stay quiet and give in to what your partner wants to avoid fighting. DON'T DO THIS. Every once in a while, you might just to make the night go by easier, but don't let this become a habit. If you do, and then you finally decide to stand up for yourself, your partner will be confused. They'll see you as combative or ask why you didn't bring things up sooner. Not wanting to fight is normal, but sometimes, it's going to happen. Fighting can actually improve your relationship way more than just keeping quiet.

Sex isn't something you should have to compromise. If you have a high libido and your partner doesn't, you might have to compromise by having less sex. Don't put pressure on someone to do something they don't want to do. If it's the opposite, however, never compromise your body just for someone else's pleasure. At one point in time, especially in the online dating world, you might meet a guy that claims he has to have sex every night in order to fall asleep. Don't buy into this. If you want to have sex every night, more power to you! Don't let your partner guilt you into having sex if you don't want to. This should never be a compromise.

Know the difference of compromising with someone and being controlled by them. Again, if you feel like you might be compromising too much, go back to the gaslighting list we had previously discussed. Is your partner saying things like that to you when you ask to get what you want? If so, it might be time for some revaluation.

Keep It 50/50

You have to remember that your lover is supposed to be a partner. They're not there to just take care of you, and you're not there to just take care of them.

50/50 means more than just splitting things in half. Picture your relationship as a cake. Let's say you've spent the day eating cake and ice cream, and your partner hasn't had cake in months. When it comes time to split the cake up, you might want to give them more slices than you'd take yourself. Does that make sense? It's not always about just cutting things down the middle. That doesn't always mean sharing. You're going to want to look at the situation as a whole and figure out how to maintain equality.

Sometimes, there might not be a balance. Maybe they're going through something hard. If they lost a family member or got laid off from their job, they're going to need you. For a while, maybe even months at a time, you're going to give 90 when they can only give 10. This is expected. The key is to make sure that things eventually go back to 50/50, and when it comes time for you to only give 10 percent, they're willing to give 90.

You shouldn't mind giving them a little bit more. This is the person that you love more than anyone. This is your life partner. Of course, you're going to want to give them more than just a little bit. If you feel as though it's been unbalanced consistently, it might be time to do some revaluation.

Be Supportive

You have to remember that the relationship isn't just about finding someone that supports you. You have to offer that same love back. Even if you might not fully believe in something they do, you should still offer the love and support needed for them to follow through with their passions.

You always have something to offer. Just because you're broke and your partner needs money to fix their problems doesn't mean you don't have anything to offer. Just letting someone know that you're there and rooting for them can be all the support they need.

It can be hard to be supportive. Sometimes you don't have the effort to support yourself, so how can you be expected to help someone else? If you feel as though you can't offer the support they deserve, let your partner know this. Say something like, "I'm sorry, I know you have a show coming up, but I just don't think I have the mental strength to go. I love you and believe in you, but I'm not emotionally available right now." Someone that loves and cares for you will understand that this is OK. It should become a consistent bad habit, but you're not going to be able to always give %100, all day every day.

Don't let them give up on their dreams. Even if they seem crazy, you should support them endlessly. If they want to become an astronaut even though they're 40 years old with no college education, tell them they can do it! They might not ever follow through, but it's still important that your partner knows that you love them endlessly.

Don't talk badly about them when they're not around. You can easily grow resentment if you spend too much time gossiping about your partner. You're going to want to gossip and vent a little bit to your girlfriends or maybe your mom. It's OK to share the small things that annoy you or even some larger fears you have. Make sure to still monitor just how much you're sharing about the other person. You don't want to grow hatred for them and make everyone around you hate them too. They're not there to defend themselves, and if you only ever share negative things about your partner with your friends, they're not going to like them either.

Don't Be Afraid to Show Affection

Don't let anyone make you feel bad about showing your partner affection and love. People sometimes get teased for showing too much PDA, but really, anyone who judges you that much has probably never had a positive relationship. We're not saying to go and make out with your partner in the middle of the grocery store. But never be afraid to give a small peck, or even hold your partner's hand. It's not silly or stupid to show someone how much you love them. It can feel good to your partner to know that you want to show them off.

Sometimes, this is the best support you can offer. If you don't have money, time, or something else they need, you always have a sweet kiss or a hug to offer them. Just these small reminders that someone else loves them can really help them through some of their darkest moments.

Human touch can cure all. If you're feeling distant from your partner, don't be afraid to tell them. Hold their hands while you have serious conversations, so they know that you still love them. Hold them while they sleep to help ease their nightmares while they're slumbering. Even a simple touch on the shoulder can really turn someone's mood around.

You don't have to be sexual to be intimate. Don't feel like kissing, making out, or cuddling has to lead to sex. These moments can actually be a little more intimate than if you did have sex. Holding each other and just feeling another person's warmth can really bring you closer.

Be respectful of others, but don't compromise when it comes to spoiling your partner. You don't want to be so obsessed with PDA that you become the couple that makes everyone uncomfortable. Just remember to never let anyone make you feel guilty about showing your partner some love.

Here are some small gestures that can really show your partner you love them.
1. Buy their favourite candy bar next time you're at the grocery store checkout
2. Highlight a part in a book you're reading that you want them to read
3. Do the dishes for them if you notice their sink is overflowing
4. Pick some wildflowers as you walk to your house. Even guys appreciate flowers every now and then!
5. Drop their favourite coffee drink off at work for them.
6. Leave post-its in their car or on their bathroom mirror that remind them how much you love them.
7. Always kiss them as you're saying hello, goodbye, goodnight, and good morning.

Chapter 8: Applying All This to Real Life

You're almost done! Once you've finished the book, it's time to start dating in the real world. We've given you a ton of information, and hopefully you've been paying attention! Taking notes is always key, and if you haven't been doing so, you haven't missed your chance yet. It can feel silly to take notes and study a book about dating. Some people feel like it's desperate or pathetic to be doing research about dating. Don't ever let anyone make you feel this way, especially yourself! It just shows that you care and that you actually want to get to know someone on a deeper level.

Reading a book is easy but putting yourself out there isn't going to be. Anyone can skim through a book and take away the important parts. Now you're going to be put to the test and you're going to have to apply all of the ideas we've discussed to your real life. It can be scary, but we're not abandoning you just yet! Here are some tips to make your transition from reader to doer!

Start Fresh with New Profiles

There is a reason that things haven't been working out so far. Maybe you've already been dating online for months now and you have yet to even go on a date. Part of it might be your own subconscious fear, but part of it might also be that you don't have a very attractive profile. Go ahead and delete all your profiles right now and start completely fresh. Rewrite your biography, take some new pictures, and just start completely over.

Instead of going back to your profiles and changing them to fit what we've talked about, don't be afraid to start fresh. It can be scary to delete different ideas, especially if you've been altering your profiles for months. Sometimes, just breathing new energy into something can be enough to make it that much more attractive. This is your time to become a new version of yourself. Leave behind the past and prepare for a brighter and better future!

Take some new pictures! You're a new person after reading this all, aren't you? We mentioned already to try and avoid selfies, but if that's all you got, that's fine too. If you're not one to take selfies, don't be afraid to let someone else take a picture of you. Next time you're at a park, walking down a cool part of the street, or getting a cup of coffee at your favourite spot, don't be afraid to ask a stranger to snap a quick picture. You'll likely never see them again, so don't be afraid to put yourself out there. Who knows, you might end up hitting it off with the person that takes your picture too! You can then use these candid's as engaging and unique profile pictures for different dating apps.

Don't google what to put in a biography. Just be true to yourself. Originality is one of the most attractive qualities. Don't put too much pressure on having something funny or witty in your biography if that's not the kind of person you are.

Be unapologetically yourself! This is the most attractive thing to other people. If you believe in yourself, so will everyone else!

Write A Letter to Yourself

We told you to write a letter to your exes to help get over them. Now it's time to write a letter to yourself. It can seem weird but grab a pen and paper and sit down to take a moment to write something to yourself, for yourself. Don't just pull out your notes app on your phone and make a list. Sit down and write a letter!

Remind yourself of how strong you are. There are going to be moments that you just want to give up but having a physical reminder you can look at will help get you through those dark periods. Remind yourself of all the great qualities you have and the people in your life that love you. No one is going to be reading this but you, so don't be afraid to go overboard. Give yourself the love you deserve! Remind yourself you're a Rockstar, a badass, a superwoman, because guess what: YOU ARE.

Writing things down can help you articulate what you're feeling. We have so many thoughts swirling through our brains at all times, that taking a moment to really write everything out can change a lot! You can keep this list around to remind you of how great you are when you're feeling down.

Oppositely, you can also write a letter to yourself about everything you hate. Write a letter saying how much you hate the way you look, or how often you feel like you embarrass yourself. It might hurt, and you might make yourself cry. Even though it's hard, do it. Once you're done with the letter, you might realize just how awful you can be to yourself. Would you give that same hateful letter to the 5-year-old version of yourself? Once you're done with the letter, rip it up, burn it, pulverise it into a bloody pulp. Whatever you do, get rid of that letter because you're done talking to yourself like that.

Make Some Lists

We've gone over a lot in this book and we've told you to do quite a few different things. You might feel overwhelmed, but that's good! This isn't going to be easy. Nothing that's worth it in the end is ever easy.

To remind you of what we've discussed in the book, here's a list of some lists that you should try writing:

1. Qualities you want in a partner.
2. Things you want out of a relationship
3. Things you admire about your family and friends
4. Things you admire about yourself
5. A list of your dreams and goals for the future (no matter how big or small)
6. Questions to ask on a first date

Chapter 9: Having Fun with It All

You're here because there's something missing in your life, right? When you see other people walking down the street and holding hands, maybe it hurts a little. Perhaps you're tired of showing up to parties and weddings alone. At the end of the night when you're laying in bed, maybe you just want someone that you can really open up to.

It's not just about sex, and it shouldn't ever be. That's certainly a great part of dating in general, but not what you should be seeking out. There are other ways to do that. You should be looking for a boyfriend, a husband, a lover, a *best friend*. Remember to stay true to that idea throughout this entire process. If you lose sight of your goal, you'll end up right where you started before you began reading this book. Never forget that at the end of the day, you're doing this for YOU.

Never Lose Yourself

You're the most important person in this entire process! If you lose yourself, or become someone completely different, what's the point? You might meet someone that you feel the need to change for. Maybe things are great at first and you just start pretending to like things you don't really care about in order to keep the peace. It might be good at first, but you never want to get in a committed relationship with someone that you have to change for. You'll never truly feel fulfilled if you allow yourself to become a different person.

If someone makes you compromise a part of you for them, they're not meant for you either. This can be a challenging thing to remember. Maybe you've been single for so long that you're desperate to keep someone around that really likes you. If you're not being authentic, however, then they still don't truly like *you*. Remember, it's better to be yourself and alone than to be living a lie with someone else.

If you let yourself become someone else and stay in a fake relationship, you'll find that you eventually become lonelier than if you never would have met anyone in the first place. True love is finding someone that you can be completely yourself with. You shouldn't have to fear what might happen if you stay true to who you are while dating another person.

Conclusion

Becoming more self-aware is one of the most important steps when starting the dating process. You are wired to be an emotional being. Your emotions are naturally ingrained into your brain to help protect you from various aspects of life. If you can learn to identify and control your emotions, you'll be surprised at just how far they can take you. Don't let your emotions dictate. It's perfectly fine to feel the way you feel, but the key is how you let your feelings control your actions. The most important thing for you to do is to take charge. You're in control! Emotions are not easy. This is probably going to be one of the most challenging things you'll have to face, but it's going to be one of the most important. Once you can do that, you can really build your confidence.

Improving your self-worth and self-esteem will help in every aspect in your life, not just your dating one. We've been taught for far too long that we're not valuable, pretty enough, skinny enough, funny enough, cool enough, and the list goes on and on. You have to always challenge these thoughts whenever you might have them and know that none of that is true! Don't say anything to yourself that you wouldn't say to an innocent person, someone like your little sibling, cousin, or even your pet. You don't deserve to be spoken down to, and that includes by yourself.

Set realistic expectations for the partner you want to find. You're not going to find someone that meets every point of your checklist. Even if you do, this might not be the person that you actually want to end up with. It's great to create a list of what you want in a partner and relationship, but you can't be too strict with that list. If you keep your vision too strict, you're going to let other things pass by that you didn't even know you needed.

Remember that you have to be attractive yourself in order to get a partner. Yes, you should always be yourself and stay true to who you are. That's something that we emphasized plenty throughout the book. Remember, however, to be the *best version* of yourself.

Online dating is scary, but it's necessary in our current world. There are plenty of people who have rejected the internet and all it has to offer, but it's a great tool to help you meet people that you wouldn't normally otherwise. There are still plenty of ways to meet people other than the internet, but don't shut this out as an option. You're going to run into some challenges when dating online, but that's inevitable. However, if you push through all the challenges you face, you just might end up meeting the love of your life.

Once you actually make it through the entire process, you can't forget how to actually maintain a healthy relationship with your partner. That's what you've worked so hard for! Remember that no time spent with anyone is a waste of time. If you've been with someone for half a decade, have a house together and maybe even a child, that doesn't mean you have to be with them forever if it isn't right. You're not obligated to make anyone happy but yourself, and you need to be sure you've entered in an equal partnership. That doesn't mean that you both have to contribute equal parts in everything you do, but just that finding the right balance for you both is the most important.

It's not going to be easy, but it's going to be the greatest thing you've ever felt. Think of the last ten songs you heard, or even the last movie you watched. There was a romance in it, right? Maybe the last song you listened to was about heartbreak, but romance was still involved. Romance novels are among the most popular books you can buy, and even the most action-packed or suspenseful TV show likely has a romantic plotline. Love is what makes the world go around. It's what keeps us getting out of bed in the morning and helps us power through our worst days. Of course, you don't need love, and loving yourself is just as important as loving your partner. If you manage to be one of the lucky ones to find love, you'll realize it's one of the greatest joys in your life. We believe that if you live true to the things we discussed in the book, you're going to find that happiness.

The most important thing to remember in this crazy process is to have fun. You're going to have moments when you want to give up. You'll likely shed some tears, maybe before you even get started. There's a chance that you might end up with a broken heart or be forced to hurt someone else (emotionally). It's not always going to be easy, but you still need to make sure that you're having fun. This shouldn't be work, and you shouldn't be torturing yourself in the process. Don't seek out a husband, look for your best friend. If someone doesn't like you or a date doesn't work out, don't blame yourself. You're going to want to do that right away, asking yourself over and over what you could have done differently. Not everyone is meant to be together, and that's OK.

One day, you're going to wake up on a weekend morning with no alarms set. The sun will be shining through the window onto you and your lover lying in bed. There's going to be a moment that they're still sleeping, and you take the chance to study their face. Watching someone you love sleep so peacefully is one of the greatest things you'll ever experience. When you make it to this moment, when you can look at someone and feel nothing but pure joy, you'll realize that everything you went through to get there was all worth it in the end.

The Social Anxiety Cure For Women Workbook

Overcome Social Anxiety Disorder, Boost Your Social Skills & Enhance Self Confidence Without Struggling From Shyness, Depression Or Self Esteem Issues

Introduction

As a student, have you ever known the correct answer to a question that your professor asked, but didn't dare answer? In the workplace, did an inspirational idea flash across your mind that you thought your colleagues or manager would love, yet you didn't feel able to share it?

Have you ever spotted an acquaintance down the street and know that they'll stop to talk to you and ask you questions, so you deliberately crossed the road to avoid them so you don't have to make small talk? Not because you dislike them at all, but simply because you feel painfully embarrassed and awkward about trying to talk to them? Do you shy away from that social situation, with every ounce of your being, so that you don't have to face questions about how things in your life are going?

Do you feel awkward in social situations where you're introduced to someone new, unsure of how to keep polite conversation going and keen for any of your friends to come and rescue you, because your friends know and understand you and don't mind that you're quiet and shy?

Do you find small talk so difficult that you'd prefer people just not talk to you at all?

Do you feel misunderstood at times? Aware that people may perceive you as being a bit standoffish, rude, or abrupt, simply because it's all you can do to utter a few words? Because your face feels hot, your hands are sweating, your chest is beating uncomfortably in situations where you feel there's too many people about who you don't know, and you're not sure what to say?

If any of these scenarios resonate with you, you're in good company.

When I was younger, these types of things happened to me on a daily basis.

These events affected me physically as well as emotionally. I would have stomach pains, rapid breathing, and excessive sweating when I was put into a situation where I felt socially awkward. Afterward, I would make myself feel physically drained by overthinking everything that I had said or ways that I'd behaved. As I experienced these feelings every day, I just assumed that life would always be like this.

My shyness expanded into full-blown anxiety. I started to worry about the mortality of those I loved and I became very close to being suicidal. I'll discuss this more in later chapters.

This book, however, isn't my biography. It is written to help you overcome shyness and have a better life!

Through the easy steps in this book, you'll learn how to get rid of your shyness and be more social and able to express yourself freely.

Regardless of what type of personality you have, this book will make you happy to be exactly who you are! You'll feel confident that you can make friends - and brave enough to express your opinions when needed.

What is This Book About?

During the first section of this book, you'll learn more about yourself and work out what is stopping you from interacting with others and expressing yourself confidently. You'll learn how changes can occur, then start to contemplate how amazing life can actually be for you.

Throughout this part of the book, I will discuss my story and explain techniques that you can try out yourself in order to make meaningful changes to your own life. The purpose of this is to let you know that everything in this book has been tried out by me, my friends, and my family members. There is solid proof that it definitely works practically and not just in theory.

In the second part of the book, you'll learn various exercises that you can immediately put into practice to develop confidence and social skills. There is a great selection of hints and tips that you can use to create conversations and build friendships. When you use a tip, you may find that this gives you a boost in confidence, you feel like you're walking on air, and you're proud of yourself. Learn to love these moments - you deserve them!

Other times, especially when you're first learning, you may feel a bit out of your depth and that it's a bit unnatural for you. That's OK, and is to be expected from time to time, but you're doing great and it will begin to flow better with time - I promise!

This book will use the phrase 'the true version of you.' What this means is that we can sometimes get taken up by fears and anxiety, or feeling judged, stressed, concerned, or as though we are unworthy or lack value. 'The true version of you' is when you naturally feel that you're accepted, content, grateful, appreciated, worthwhile, and calm. This is the person you would be if you didn't have any fears, any worries, or any beliefs about how others are viewing or judging you. This is you without a care in the world, able to just express every thought in your head clearly without any limits. This doesn't mean you'll turn into a brash, verbally-blundering oaf without tact or diplomacy - but simply that any time you want to speak socially, you are able to say what you want to express clearly and politely.

'The true version of you' holds no religious connotations. It simply means a state wherein you're happy and content with exactly who you are.

Chapter 1 - The Prison of Fear

There's a quote by David Icke which says, "The greatest prison people live in is the fear of what other people think."

Lots of people have opinions about all sorts of things, but this doesn't make them an expert in the area. People are entitled to have certain viewpoints on matters, but it doesn't make them right. It is daft to worry about other people's opinions, and even more so to worry about speaking to others in case they don't approve of what we have to say.

Most people won't judge you or be as critical of you as you fear they will be. If people are, then it's quite possible they don't have a good understanding of you. Don't live in a prison of fear, worrying about other people's opinions.

When I was younger, I loved sports. Swimming was one of my favourites, because there's not much of a chance for conversation when people are mostly submerged in water. I did quite well with it. I also liked football, basketball, and baseball because they were all quite active. I became engrossed in the game, worrying about running and moving, rather than stressing about communicating with others. After high school, I chose to go to a very sports-oriented University.

I had, however, changed from simply feeling shy to experiencing a more extreme anxiety. I chose to avoid University dormitories. Instead, I decided to live with some of my high school friends. I had successfully managed to avoid mixing with large numbers of new people. I did participate in partying and I didn't study as much as I should have. I was drinking to avoid acknowledging the thoughts that were plaguing my mind. Drinking gave me false courage and allowed me to be more extroverted and chat with others. But I was living with fear - and drinking to excess. This wasn't good for my health, and I'll discuss this more in later chapters.

It is important to understand why we have the fears that we do. By understanding them, we can then more easily tackle them.

Fear and Shyness are Best Friends

Fear can be a sensible reaction. Fear is in our DNA from ancient ancestors, such as Neanderthals, who needed to know to run from woolly mammoths to stay alive. It was also important to remain part of a social group in order to have food, shelter, and to ward off predators.

In today's society, we still have fear. And some of this fear still relates to being part of certain groups - or feeling rejected from those groups. Rejection is a key aspect of fear. If we're rejected today, nothing will happen to us and we aren't in any danger. But we still associate rejection with loss and death. While rejection is unpleasant and upsetting, it isn't going to be a matter of life or death. It can just make us feel a bit rubbish.

In today's society, we feel rejection in many different ways. For example, we invite someone on a date, have to give a presentation, attend a job interview, or answer the phone. We fear that the person will say no to the date; we fear that the people we're presenting to won't like us or enjoy the presentation; we fear we won't get the job; we fear that people won't be able to understand us on the phone or will talk too quickly or quietly to be understood, etc.

This fear is inside us. If you're a shy person, you most likely have an overactive imagination. This can be a good thing and can make you very creative. But, it can also be detrimental to your well-being as you'll imagine the very worst-case scenarios and remember everything negative that has ever happened in the past.

But, you are in control of your imagination. You are in charge here. Instead of remembering everything bad that has happened previously, you can imagine yourself interacting well with people. If you have been worried about reacting in an interview, you can set the scene in your head of you walking in with confidence, shaking their hands, and creating a lasting impression of someone who is confident and in control.

When we're fearful, adrenaline kicks in and we're in fight or flight mode. We need to take the fight from the adrenaline and use it to destroy any fear.

Internal Critic vs. Living in the Present

When I was at College, I attended a drama class. I felt very daring attending a class that made me feel uncomfortable and took me out of my comfort zone. I did learn a really valuable lesson from the professor though that has helped me throughout life.

Each student was asked to give two 60-second presentations to the rest of the class about his/her background. On the first presentation, the person had a mirror that reflected their face for the entire minute. It was awkward for both the presenter and the audience.

When it was my turn, I was very aware of my appearance - my hair, my mouth as I spoke, etc.

When we each presented again, without the mirror, it was a far more pleasant experience for all involved - far more relaxed and fluid - even enjoyable!

When the mirror was there, we had a tendency to be focused on ourselves and worry about others' perceptions of us. We viewed ourselves harshly and worried about criticism. We were concerned with examining ourselves with internal, critical thoughts.

But, when we did not have the mirror, we were able to be ourselves, look at the audience and interact with them more freely.

If you spend too much time with your 'internal critic,' you're unable to live in the present moment.

If, when someone is having a conversation with you, you're constantly worrying about what your reply will be, then you're not truly listening to them. You're spending time with your 'internal critic,' rather than them.

Chapter 2 - Opportunity

So, returning to the story of when I was at University and drinking way too much.

I woke up one morning, after a night of heavy drinking, and I felt really unhappy with myself. I played back everything I'd said the night before and was astounded at how stupid I'd been. (In reality, I probably hadn't said many silly things. I was just over-analysing and being hyper-critical of myself. Anyone else who had been there wouldn't have thought anything of the events at all). But, I spent the morning beating myself up about all the ridiculous things I thought I had said.

I felt like I needed a change of scenery, so I walked around the halls. But, all I felt was a sense of regret for everything I'd said the night before. I despised my actions and speech. I was also suffering with a hangover from too much alcohol. I took myself off for a walk.

I felt like I wasn't in control over how I was behaving.

I walked to a bridge and stood there for a long time, watching the water below, and the thought truly crossed my mind: *What if I decided to just jump, and fall towards the water?*

I couldn't tell if I was still drunk from the night before. I'd never even thought about such a thing before. But, the worrying thing was that it was quite appealing to me; it would stop me thinking about all of the awful thoughts in my mind.

Thankfully, I broke out of this mood and realised that would be stupid. I took myself away from the danger of the bridge. I realised that there is ALWAYS something to live for, that life does indeed get better, and that my parents, family, and friends would be devastated if I killed myself. If you're ever feeling low and depressed or suicidal, consider family, friends, and people who rely on you (including pets who are dependent on your love and care). Think about seeing beautiful sunsets and sunrises, and of experiencing the sensation of the drizzle of rain on your skin. There are people who you have not yet met, but who will in the future impact your life and be so significant to you - and you to them - that you need to carry on living in order to meet them. There are things you can do throughout the course of your life that will make a true difference to others, whether that's volunteering, helping someone with words or writing, doing a gesture of kindness such as buying someone lunch or a coffee, or just listening. You are living your life for a purpose, even if you're not sure of that yet.

But, the very fact I'd even thought about committing suicide really scared me. I understood that I drastically needed to change things in my life to prevent myself from being in the same spot a few weeks down the line.

A few weeks later, I saw an advert for a self-help book by Vinny Guadagnino called *Control the Crazy*. I downloaded the book from Amazon and the stories in the book really resonated with me. I found that I just kept on reading and nodding in agreement with the situations that Vinny described. It made me very aware that there were other people who felt exactly like I did. I had felt alone, like no-one was experiencing what I did, and that I didn't really belong in the world. It was reassuring that other people had felt like me, and had gotten over that and were now living happy lives. If they could, so could I.

Changing my Mind

The book mentioned that every individual has 60,000 thoughts a day. I was astounded at this. I then jolted to Earth with a bump when I realised that three-quarters of my thoughts were quite negative and very anxious: worrying that I was shy; believing there to be something the matter with me; worrying about what I had said; wishing I was more confident; being envious of people who were, etc.

But then I thought, if Vinny, the author of the book, had felt just like me and managed to change, well then so could I! I simply needed to follow in his footsteps. There are many techniques I embarked upon:

- Yoga
- Meditation
- Compiling a 'thankful' journal
- Healthy eating
- Counselling
- Reading self-help books

I would also use visualisation techniques, imagining myself confident and no longer shy. It was great to be that free. The imagination is a truly wonderful thing. It's a bit like a call-out to the Universe about what you want. With time, the Universe has a great way of obliging and trying to get for you what you imagine. You clearly play a role in this too, but don't get too hung up about 'how' it'll happen, and trust that it will. If you imagine yourself being able to speak in social situations confidently and having a group of friends who are supportive, loyal, and fun to be around, chances are that in a short while, this will be the case.

I wanted to develop myself and have more power over my emotions and mind. I began to learn that this was definitely possible to do.

My life, from the outside, may have looked quite similar to how it previously had to other people. But I was beginning to feel different and better myself. A change was occurring.

Fulfilling My Abilities

Despite different socioeconomic backgrounds, opportunities, and education, each person can decide to shape themselves into whatever they want to become.

It may seem that some people struggle more than others. Some people may seem more confident, whilst others may seem more shy.

But, Tony Robbins gives good advice in his 'success cycle' of 'potential' – 'action' – 'belief' and 'result.'

It is possible for this cycle to perpetuate both positively and negatively.

For example, if you believe you only have the 'potential' to be shy, you may believe that you're shy, and this is how it will be all of your life. Your 'action,' because you believe you are shy, may be to avoid talking with new people or expressing yourself. The 'result' would be that you feel awkward and don't know how to behave socially around people. The 'belief' would be that you reinforce your own behaviour and say, "See, I told you so!"

Visualise the Changes you Want to See

You many get to a point which feels like your lowest ebb, and decide that you've had enough and need to make changes. You already have the answers to all your issues and problems. You need to identify them - then tackle them.

One key technique is for you to use visualisation to imagine how your future will be. Instead of having worrying, negative images, you'll create and imagine fantastic, positive ones. Believing that something is possible is more than half-way toward achieving it.

The runner, Roger Bannister, believed he could run a mile in less than four minutes. Prior to 1954 no one had managed to do this. But, he constantly visualised himself achieving this goal; and he did. People after that have done the same.

Allow yourself to be open to fulfilling your abilities. Allow yourself to imagine how it would feel being who you want to be.

This has been scientifically proven to work. If you spend 5-10 minutes each day visualising yourself as confident and chatting with people easily, it will become significantly easier for this to become a reality. It's like rehearsing for a theatre performance in your mind; you've already prepared yourself for how it will feel.

Chapter 3 – Change

Approximately half a year after reading the book, *Control the Crazy*, my life still looked similar to how it had prior to reading it.

Because I'd started living in a healthier way, I was beginning to feel a little better. I wasn't drinking anywhere near as much, and I spent more time studying. These were small, positive changes that made a difference, but I was still uncomfortably shy.

At this point, I wasn't aware that there was going to be a change in my life.

As it neared the summer holiday, most of my friends returned to their families and jobs. Because I had failed a number of classes at University, I stayed in order to do resits, study, and continue working at a center on campus.

It dawned on me that unless I made the effort to make some friends, spend 12 weeks just watching reruns on the TV and playing computer games.

Then, the change occurred.

It seemed like a normal day. In my job, I was going through my usual tasks; and then, almost like a rush of warmth through my body, I suddenly started talking to my colleagues and customers.

I was able to be cheerful and attentive, joke, listen well and respond accordingly; and I was beginning to develop friendships. It was the best feeling ever!

I didn't know what had happened.

Usually, after a conversation, I'd sit and analyse every aspect of who had said what. But instead, I just decided to go with it.

My shift at work went by at lightning speed, and it was soon nearing home-time. I didn't want to go home from work. This was the most fun I'd had in weeks.

When I did get home, it felt almost as though someone had cast a magic spell over me. I felt amazing. It was great having good conversations with people. I knew that this was a dramatic change and turning point in my life. It was going to be addictive.

The remainder of the summer was a great period of change for me. I viewed every single day as a chance to speak to someone new, learn something new, and overcome my shyness. I made so many friends in my resit classes and at work. These had been people who I'd seen plenty of times in the past but had previously been worried about chatting with.

I attended social functions, had a fun time, and managed to curb how much alcohol I drank. I explored the city where I worked; and that was fun. I approached summer by being accepting of suggestions and trying new things. I felt as though life was new and exciting; and I loved having good conversations with the people around me.

I enjoyed both work and my studies, and felt motivated and interested in both. There was a real transformative change in how I felt - from feeling shy, odd, not fitting in, and being perceived as the strange person in a group - to feeling that life is way too short to hide away or to worry excessively about other people's opinions. I felt that I wanted to make the most of every opportunity and to take every chance I could to talk to and learn from others.

I truly believed that I could get over being shy. And I felt that being shy had made me miss out on so many things in life up until this point. I was always a little envious of my father, who was a bubbly person who loved being around others and was the life and soul of every event. He had a good group of friends, who he often spent time with, and they really enjoyed his company. I had often wished I was like him, and it was only now that I started to think I could be.

Because I knew I was well on my way to overcoming the fear and shyness, I knew that I could tackle anything else in my life that was a fear. I figured that if I could overcome the anxiety that had dominated my life, then I could do pretty much anything that I set my mind to. Anything which in the past had been a barrier, I now brought to the surface and viewed as an opportunity to change in order to make myself stronger and better.

I had previously really wanted to study sports at College but did not have the faith in myself that I was good enough at it. I had also given up the one sport I was good at as a child for another, that I wasn't so good at. I went from being a strong swimmer to being a poor basketball player. I didn't look like a basketball player and I didn't play well. I spent most of my time senior year sitting on the bench.

But, I did know I had been good at swimming. Believing now that anything is possible, I couldn't help but ponder how good I'd need to get at it again in order to be accepted at College. It began to filter through my mind often and it was something I couldn't stop daydreaming about.

Your Change

So, you may be thinking that this is great news for me as author of this book. But, you bought this book because you wanted to stop being shy. And you may still be wondering how this will take place for you.

Well, whatever it is that you want to overcome, whether that is to become less shy, to improve how you communicate with others, or to feel freer to express exactly what you want to say without fear of other people's opinions, it is a 'change' that will enable this to occur.

Before we look further at how you can bring about this change, I want to emphasize - this book is about you being proactive and doing something to create change. If you don't do that, but simply keep reading self-help book after self-help book, attending seminars, and listening to webinars on self-improvement, you'll just spend your life searching for the answer. And you actually already know the answer and what needs to be done. Let's make this happen.

What is a 'Change'?

A change is that moment when you say to yourself, "Enough is enough. Something needs to change and be different from before." There is that old adage, "If you always do what you've always done, you will always get what you've always got." It works for many things in life, such as if you've always started a diet then a day into it, found yourself binge-eating packets of crisps and biscuits, you're always going to remain unhappy with the weight you are. If you're single, and fed up of being so, but never leave the house in order to meet someone new and never participate in any online dating sites, well then, you're probably going to remain unhappy and single. You need to make a change, whether it means that you eat more healthily and exercise if you want to lose weight, or that you go out more or join online dating sites if you want to meet a partner. If you want to make a change regarding your shyness, you need to take action, too, and speak more. There are lots of techniques in the second half of this book that will help you learn how to speak to others with ease; and I promise you that you will find it much easier than you expect.

It is highly likely that you have experienced change in your life. It could be that you've decided to give up smoking or stop eating chocolate. Or perhaps you've had a fall out with someone and later decided to let bygones be bygones and move on from that. Whatever that moment was, there was a change; and your life is different and hopefully better because of it.

The Strengths and Limits of Your Beliefs

In our own minds, we each hold beliefs about the type of person we are and what we think we're capable of achieving. To have this type of mental conversation with yourself doesn't make you insane - it's what everyone does. This type of belief system, though, shapes how you interact with the world.

This book will definitely give you hints, tips, techniques, and practical actions you can carry out which will enable you to become less shy and speak to people with confidence. But, if your belief system is constantly saying to you, "This is mumbo jumbo, and it doesn't really work," then you may remain a shy person - at least until you change how you think. Have faith that this book will work for you and I can 100% promise you that it will. It has worked for me; it has worked for my friends; and it's worked for other people who have read the book and followed the hints and tips and put them into practice.

The key difference between those who feel shy, awkward, and like they don't belong, compared to those who are confident, outgoing and fit in with people from all walks of life, is simply accounted for by the beliefs that each person has about themselves. My Dad, who is a very confident man, has a positive outlook on life. When he goes out, he expects that other people will like his company and find him interesting and funny; and they do. He never has any hesitance in this belief. He doesn't worry that people may think him silly or will be critical of what he has to say, whereas I previously had worried constantly about these type of things.

What are your beliefs? Do they boost your confidence and make you feel good about yourself? Or do they drag you down? Do your self-beliefs make you feel as though you are brimming with energy, or make you want to go to bed and just pull a big duvet around you? If your closest friend said the same things to you that you're telling yourself, would you still be friends with them? You need to learn to be as kind to yourself with your internal voice as you would be to one of your friends.

As mentioned earlier, the beliefs I had about myself were: I lack confidence; I'm odd; I find it hard to make small talk; I feel self-conscious and in the way or out-of-place; I don't fit in. I'd worry about talking in case everyone thought my ideas were ridiculous. Whether these were true was entirely my choice. My beliefs became true by me acting them.

To change the beliefs I held about myself, I used a technique learned from meditation. I would internally examine all the beliefs and thoughts I had, in little cloud-shaped bubbles. If the thought was a good thought and boosted my self-esteem, the cloud bubble was allowed to stay. If it wasn't a good thought, then I was let the cloud bubble float away out of my ear.

We become what we think of ourselves.

Instead of focusing on the negative: "I don't want to be shy," you need instead to focus on what you do want. Saying "I don't want to be shy," almost works as an affirmation that you're a shy person and you believe it. Instead, try changing the way you think to, "I want to be bubbly and confident with lots of friends." This is a much more positive cloud to have in your head, and to keep there, without it needing to float out of your ear.

This isn't just wishy-washy, self-help, positive-thinking rubbish. It works in an ingrained psychological way.

In a similar way to how our beliefs shape how we view ourselves and others, how we feel energy-wise has an impact on our real-life experiences.

If you feel shy and timid, you'll talk yourself out of acting confidently in conversations.

We will use the analogy of a thermostat for the way you think. Now, let's assume that over time, you have become comfortable with the thermostat set to 72 degrees. Each day, your temperature will be affected by good things that make the temperature increase, and bad things that make the temperature reduce. But, with time, you find your way back to the 72 degrees where you're most comfortable.

When you're trying to be less shy and need greater energy to do this, you'll need to adjust your thermostat to around 75 degrees, initially. This will require effort on your part because you'll be unused to it being so warm, and you will feel a little uncomfortable until you are accustomed to it.

But what you need to note is that it's you who is in full control of the thermostat.

You can control your energy using your body. You can change how you feel by how much you move and how active you are. We all know that we can tone our bodies, develop muscles, and create endorphins when we exercise.

It's not necessary to exercise directly before engaging in conversation. But, doing some exercise each day will make your mind much more active and open, too. If we mentally try to persuade ourselves to do something, it can be really hard to get motivated. But, if we physically move ourselves, it will give more energy and positivity to our minds too, and give us much more willpower and determination.

You need to start monitoring your energy levels. When they reduce, you need to find a way to increase them, as it happens.

The Optimum Moment

Your 'change' will occur when your mind is energized, active, and open, and when your beliefs are positive and you're mentally excited about what the future holds. This will be your optimum moment, when all the pieces fit together. Something will trigger this, and it can work in odd ways. Sometimes it can be when things have gone well and you're encouraged to push yourself to move onto something new. At other times, when things seem bad, it can be the catalyst for change. It can be a point of, 'Something needs to change now,' or, 'Things are at rock bottom. There's only one way to go from here, and that's up.'

This optimum moment of transitional change will occur one day. You dictate when this change happens. You can decide to make that change right now. Or, wait until a year down the line when you decide to change then. The decision is entirely yours. But I would encourage you to make the change as soon as you feel you possibly can, because your life will be so much better. The very first time you apply one of these techniques from the back of the book, you will be glowing with pride in yourself for days. And this glow will portray you as being happier, more confident and content, and will attract more people to you.

The very first time I tried the technique was when I went to a music gig with my partner. The musicians from the gig, after performing, mingled with the audience. I'd seen a musician and wanted to talk to him - and I plucked up the courage to do so. I wasn't awe-struck. I spoke sensibly to him about his previous occupation and managed to end the brief conversation with a polite, "It's been nice to meet you." But the fact that I'd plucked up the courage to do this made me smile for days afterwards, every time I thought of it. I could see the look of surprise on my partner's face when they saw I was talking to someone, because I was usually so shy. My partner even took a photo of me chatting. I was pleased when I saw in the photo that I was holding my hands in an appropriate place as I chatted, and I was smiling and looking interested. All of these aspects of poise will be discussed later in the second half of the book. I did it - and so can you.

Chapter 4 – Growing Yourself

So far, the book has discussed changes that you'll make and actions you'll take to become less shy. Change happens, regardless of whether we want it to sometimes. But, the key thing here is growing yourself so that you're more who you should be, who you were meant to be, and who you would be if you were free from the many constraints that society places on us and the barriers we have built up around ourselves.

There is nothing wrong with you at all. And don't for one moment think that there is. This book isn't about you 'changing' who you are as a person because there is nothing wrong with with you as you are. It's about you growing and developing as a person to become the best version of you that you can be.

When you grow into the person you are, you'll become friendlier and enjoy conversing with others. And you'll be prepared to be sillier and less concerned about letting your reserved barriers down. You'll feel free to express what you're passionate about - your interests and hobbies. You won't be shy and quiet about these or worried that others won't find these interesting. When you talk about things you're interested and enthusiastic about, this excitement will rub off on others. If you speak quickly, timidly, or with reservation, about a topic, people won't find this as stimulating as someone who can barely control their excitement. You need to understand your fears first of all, and you need to experience that instant when you'll change.

When that summer was approaching its close, I decided to make some plans for the future. I dared to imagine what it was in life that I desired, and this was a new thing for me.

I wasn't sure of exactly how all this would occur yet. But, what I did know was:

1. I wanted some sort of new experience
2. I wanted to do swimming at College

3. I wanted to live in a warm environment

I was very excited and hopeful - and my answer came to me. I decided to move away from home and go to a school in Southern California. It was like a clean slate for me; a brand-new start. I was free to create a life for myself, exactly of my own choosing. This was what I wanted, and this is what I did. I was determined that this should be my course of action and I did everything I could to make it happen. Just four weeks later, I'd packed all my belongings in my case and was ready to set off in my car on my next life adventure.

Liberating Being Me

Happiness.

Happiness and contentment ran through my veins as I drove for two days to my new life in Southern California. It was a wonderful road trip. I enjoyed driving; I had the car windows open, a breeze blew in, providing some relief from the heat, and I had my favourite music on. It made me feel as happy and carefree as I'd been as a child.

As I drove, the concept of a 'clean slate' really appealed to me. No one knew me in Southern California. I didn't have any excess baggage, with people perceiving me as the 'shy one,' or the 'nerdy one,' or the 'odd one who never really fit in.' If you're in a place where everyone knows you, it can feel harder to suddenly decide to dress or act differently, because you'll have people seeing how different it is. However, they would soon get over it and adapt to the new version of you. Moving isn't always the answer, or the only option. In Southern California, I was free to create my own identity exactly as I chose. I could decide to act and behave exactly how I wanted to there, and people would just assume that's how I'd always been. I was thrilled, and it just felt amazing!

Have you ever felt like that?

It is a wonderful thing to realize that you can create this clean slate, this new start for yourself at any point you want to. You don't have to move schools or locations to make it happen. The only thing you do need is to make the decision to change and have the determination to stick to it. People around you who know you may be a little shocked or surprised upon the first instance of you suddenly becoming chatty, confident, and outgoing. But if you keep on doing that, this will become the new perceived impression of you. When someone is confident, it can be a little disarming because it gives a person poise and shows contentment and total happiness, but it's also very appealing and nice to be around. It can put others at ease, too.

At University, I settled into my accommodation, then I immediately became involved in mixing with the people around me. Some of this was driven by anxiety. I was more concerned with not having a group of friends than people disliking me. So, I tried really hard to make friends wherever I went.

Within just 2 weeks of being there, I gained a position on the swim team, joined the student government, and gained employment working on the reception desk of the student accommodation. My key motivation with all three of these was to make friends and enjoy myself as much as I could. That's a really nice approach when you start anything new, whether that's a sport, a group, or a job. Wanting to meet new people and find out about what they have to say and the things you can learn from them, and wanting to having fun and enjoy yourself is a very positive way of life. You'll see the best in people, be friendly, smile, and joke; and you will attract all this back to you. You'll be a fun person to be around and you'll find yourself invited to more social functions. It's a circle whereby you'll constantly expand your group of friends.

I pretended that I was a social, outgoing person, and had always been; and it became reality. It was very natural and didn't take any effort.

As it happened, I was only able to stay at that school for a semester, so I had just three months there. This was because I couldn't get the money to cover the fees going forward. But, I shall always look back very fondly on that time as being significant in my development.

During that time, I made friends who I'm still in contact with today. I achieved my dream of being a college athlete. I was no longer stilted by my fears or anxieties, but faced these head on. I was very happy and at ease with life.

One of the key things that I took from this was that I discovered I could be enthusiastic and passionate about things in a way that I never realised I could be. I would never have realised that I had this kind of drive in me if I hadn't pushed myself into a place beyond my comfort zone.

If you want to be a confident person and achieve certain aims in life, at times you will need to step outside of your comfort zone and move into places where you stand the chance of rejection. But you will certainly develop and grow from your experience.

There's a book called *One Minute Millionaire* wherein the author, Robert Allen says, "Everything you want in your life is just outside your comfort zone."

When you push yourself to a place beyond where you're comfortable, you may feel a bit odd and awkward at first, but this is the place where magical things happen. It's similar to when you're brave enough to enter the sea. The water may feel cold at first, but you soon acclimate to it and enjoy splashing around, it feels vibrant and exciting.

This is similar to stepping into a new area out of your comfort zone and becoming closer to your true self.

One evening a week, I was asked to give a small talk about my experiences by the Student Body President. The idea initially terrified me - which is why I decided to go ahead and do it. I was out of my comfort zone and I realised this was good for me.

As I gave my little talks each week, I shared information about deciding to move to California. I had never felt more alive than I did when giving these talks, and I realised that I was motivated by my ability to inspire other people through my stories.

Previously, if anyone had suggested that each week, I'd standing in front of a group, confidently talking about myself, I would have thought they were completely deluded. This would have terrified me in the past. But, I knew the group was friendly and genuinely had an interest in hearing from me, so I thought I'd give it a go. With time, upon giving the talks, I felt more and more confident. People listened; they were interested and would ask questions afterwards. People thanked me for the talks and told me how much they'd enjoyed them or how they'd helped them.

It could be that you already have a very clear idea about what you want to do with your life. Or, you may feel that you're just going through the motions of life, with no clear idea of direction. You may feel stuck in a rut, like everyone seems to be making progress in life - bar you, that time is just standing still for you. Being stuck is a horrible feeling, because you find it hard to see how you're going to get past this brief phase, and how life will be any different from this in the future. But, you will. Life will get better; this is just a blip.

If it is simply your shyness that you feel is preventing you from being your true self, then this needs to be worked on right now. You need to let the person trapped inside your shy exterior escape and be free. You have the power and ability to do this. I know; I have been exactly where you are right now, and I've escaped. And it's the best thing that has ever happened to me, which is why I'm encouraging you to do the same.

Think briefly of your very worst-case scenario… Imagine you're in a bar and don't know anyone at all. Imagine you pluck up the courage to go up and chat with a group of girls and say, "I wondered if you'd mind if I joined you for a short while. I don't know anyone here. Would that be OK?" In the worst-case scenario that the girls sniggered and said something like, "Actually, no. We want to be on our own," what's the worse that happens? You may feel that they were a bit rude. You may feel a little hurt and a bit rebuffed. But, IF that happened - and that's a big 'If' - that says more about the group of girls than it does you. It shows they're not very welcoming and not very friendly; but, it says nothing bad about you. You've been polite, open, honest, and friendly – and those are all really good qualities. If they giggle, they may be doing so out of awkwardness or immaturity, or they could be just being mean. It still doesn't say anything bad about you. Whilst you may feel slightly rejected... That's the worst that happens. You don't die! You live another day. You dust yourself off and realise this is actually a good thing. You've learned quickly that they're not your type of people. You move on from them, ideally that very same night, until you meet people who are better aligned with you. I actually think the chances of being rebuffed by a group are very slim. Most people, if approached in the right way, will welcome you into the group, make introductions, and do their best to include you in conversations and make you feel at ease.

Making the Most of Your Abilities

Your aim is to be more confident with a bubbly personality. To start this, you need to believe that you will be more confident and visualise yourself being more confident and less shy. I'm one hundred percent positive that you have hidden abilities and expertise that you may not have even realized. I believe that every single person has a special skill or ability, something that they're talented at, that makes them stand out from the crowd. Everyone has strengths - things they're good at. If you're unsure what it is, start by thinking about what you most enjoy doing. Generally, people enjoy the things that they're good at because it comes naturally to them.

One of the key ways that your life can be more exciting and special to you is to set yourself aims and decide to make a change.

If you spend too much time dwelling on how shy you are, you'll trap yourself with negative self-belief and won't be able to move from that position. You'll think that you're shy, and therefore will act in a shy way, avoiding conversation, not chipping in with opinions but rather keeping them to yourself. You'll avoid social functions and will miss out on a lot. When you believe something about yourself, you then tend to act in this way. It's a self-fulfilling prophecy. You'll become stuck and stagnant in life.

What you need to do instead is focus on how you'd like your life to be; the universe and our own minds will find a way to make this happen. When you're thinking about an ideal world, if you could be anything, do anything, and have life exactly how you consider to be perfect, what do you see? Now think about it again, but ensure that you pack the image with as many details, colours, and textures as possible. You need to really bring this daydream to life in your mind. Make it as vibrant as and as realistic as you can. Think often about this.

My life changed dramatically once I started to talk more confidently to others. I followed a route of acting how I wanted to behave and trusting that this would work; it did. I know that this can work for you, too.

Setting Great Goals

Toward the end of this chapter, I'm going to encourage you to really talk to your inner child and allow yourself to dream with no barriers at all. Absolutely anything is possible in this exercise. You don't have to be bound by what is 'realistic'; just simply dream. To truly get inspiration and be inventive and creative, you have to dream big without any limitations. Many people who have created new inventions did so by allowing themselves to dream big with no limits, then worked out later how the dream could be achieved. Many people who have started new businesses again allowed themselves to dream big initially, then worked out a little later what was immediately feasible and what would have to wait until a little later.

This is a wonderful, enjoyable thing to do. But firstly, you need to ensure that you're in the best possible mood for this to work as well as it can. You need to be feeling energetic and filled with enthusiasm before starting this task. If you need to do some physical exercise in order to get yourself pumped up, and the adrenaline running, then do so.

The next thing to do is to take a notepad and a pen and write out 50 goals! These can be any type of short-term or long-term goals to do with health, fitness, hobbies, your career, spirituality, finances, or any other goals you may have.

Because the key aim of this book is for you to be more social and confident, that should certainly be one of the goals you include on your list. So, your aims could include being more confident, less shy, able to speak in front of groups, able to express your views, and to be a person who is content with their life and does not feel like they're being held back in any way.

Try not to stop writing goals until the 30 minutes is up. If you have more than 50 in that time, that's great! If you don't yet have 50, then take a bit more time until you have reached the 50 mark. I swiftly managed to write around 40. The last 10 were a little harder for me to think of - but, I soon got there. This is a great exercise for focusing your mind on what is important to you. You may find on your list some goals that you 'think' you should have, either because this is what your family expects of you or what society thinks should be goals for people. But later, when you come to prioritise those goals in the next step, do ensure it is YOUR goals that you're prioritising - what YOU really want, not what is expected of you by others.

Next, from your list of 50, ensure you have the top 5 goals that you're most passionate about. When you're enthusiastic and excited about your goals, that lets you know that these are the correct things that you should be focussing on in life. At least one of these goals should be a goal that relates to being less shy, more confident, and more social.

The next step is that you need to search the Internet or magazines to find pictures that represent what success in these goals looks like to you. So if, for example, one of your goals/aims was to dress better, you could find images of the type of clothes, shoes, and accessories that you'd like to wear. Over time, finances permitting, you can gradually add items to your wardrobe so that you can make this a reality.

If your goal was to have a nice circle of friends, you could find images of groups of friends enjoying various activities together, such as: meals out; meals cooked at one another's homes; trips to the theatre or cinema; game nights; day trips to new places; BBQs in the summer; evenings by the bonfire; Halloween or Christmas together; baby-showers; cafes for tea and cakes; playing golf; attending gigs; weddings; walks etc. - whatever it is that you like to do, and would like to spend time with friends doing.

If you're determined to make friends and have a nice social circle, you will. Remember though that friendship takes work. You can't always wait for people to contact you to ask if you'd like to do something. If they have contacted you though, try to make time to spend time with them. Everyone has busy lives, juggling work and family commitments and various other activities, but try to spend time chatting, have cups of tea/cake, have a pint at a local pub, or a game of golf, etc. Check in on your friends from time to time, to ask how they are and invite them places.

Don't be hurt or take it to heart if they don't want to go where you invite them, or aren't able to. They will also lead busy lives and be juggling many things. What you can do is try to have a fairly open invitation rather than to a specific set event, where you say, "Would you be free to meet up any time from X date onwards? I can't do X, Y or Z, but I'm free at other times." This gives your friends a clear chance, which is as open as possible, to check their diaries and schedules and find a convenient time. If they're not free, then ask them to suggest an alternative date/s to see how that works for you. It's nice to have dates to meet up with friends scheduled for the future as it will give you something to look forward to. And it's always nice to chat with others and find out about their lives and learn something new.

So, these 'ideal' and 'perfect' images you've found of how you'd like your life to be, taken from either magazines or the Internet - you need to bring these images to life and have daily reminders of them. You can either print these images out or create cards with them to make a vision board that you can look at to what you want in the future. The brighter and more colourful the better, as it's easier to visualise. I like the idea of a vision board, and it works well for me personally, because often some of your goals are linked and it's nice to be able to cast your eyes over all your goals at once and to have these easy to see.

The next step is to attach an affirmation to each of these images, as though you have achieved the goal and you're living with that achievement every day. The more detailed you can be about exactly what it is that you desire, the easier your mind will find the answers and make it happen. Use confident language in your affirmations and say things such as, 'I am outgoing, sociable, and bubbly with lots of friends.'

You need to look at these goals every day. You need to believe that they are already true each time. You need to use your imagination to put yourself into situations where you act out what would be your desired result and prepare yourself like a dress-rehearsal for when this is true in your day-to-day life. When you set a goal, it can often be more about the journey to the goal than the goal itself. In the process of reaching your goal, you become a different person. Every single time that you look at the images, and read the affirmations connected to them, you'll feel enthusiastic about imagining that situation as though it was a reality. When you read your affirmations, ideally aloud, be as energetic, passionate, and brimming with enthusiasm as you can. Every day, have your vision board or notecards in sight so that you see them, especially first thing in the morning and before you go to bed, and have these images firmly in your mind.

You may not understand currently why you're working on goal setting when this book is about you becoming less shy and more sociable. It's sensible to ask. But, like a smoker who finds it difficult to cease smoking until they partake in a new habit that distracts them from smoking, you will not overcome shyness until you become so focussed on working towards your aims and goals that you'll be too busy - and too involved in and passionate about your goals - to care about being shy.

This may sound odd, but I have lived through this experience and know it to be true. I know that if it was the case for me, it'll be the same for you, also.

You need to have goals and look at them daily.

Chapter 5 – Be Realistic and Honest with Yourself

This is the point of your life where you need to be realistic about yourself as a person. In order for me to get to the point where I decided to overcome my shyness, I spent a long time writing in a journal, read self-help books, and had regular meetings with a counsellor.

Each time I met with a counsellor, it gave me a feeling of relief and freedom. It was only with the counsellor that I felt comfortable sharing information about myself that I hadn't shared previously with my closest friends and family. It was important for me to speak with a complete stranger, because otherwise I may have been worried about being so open and honest and may have not wanted to hurt my friends or family's feelings. Therefore, I wouldn't have said everything that was on my mind. It's great to have the ability to speak freely, and be listened to, in a completely non-judgemental way, with no fear of upsetting someone.

Right here and now, let everything out!

How to Express Yourself Freely

2 key ways that stand out are:

1. Having professional counselling
2. Writing your feelings in a notebook

If you don't feel that you want to talk to a person about how you feel, then writing your thoughts will work just as well, only it's cheaper and you can do it from the comfort of your own home, at any time that is convenient to you!

Set a stopwatch for half an hour and write anything that is on your mind. Absolutely anything. Do not stop writing until the 30 minutes are up. I would advise you to do this on notebook paper using a pen or pencil, rather than typing these electronically. Try to do this every single day - but at a minimum you should be aiming for three times a week.

When you maintain a notebook or journal of your thoughts, feelings, dreams, impressions, and experiences, it's a great way to keep track of them. It allows you to organize them and become clearer about them. This can lead to dramatic insights, which can have an impact upon future thoughts and behaviour. A journal should contain a description of what has happened as well as your thoughts and musings about it.

What is great about keeping a journal is that it's only you who will read this. You're not writing for an audience, so it doesn't have to make sense to anyone but you. You can ignore any spelling mistakes, grammatical errors, any issues with your order, or whether it is easily understood. You can be one-hundred percent open and honest and not worry about hurting anyone's feelings or making a fool of yourself. You can be as creative as you want with it. If you are writing content that could potentially be misunderstood by family members, then try to ensure you keep your journal hidden away somewhere safe when it's not in use, so that it isn't easily accessible.

Your journal can be used as a key way of understanding yourself. Life today is busy and fraught with pressures. A journal gives you an opportunity to slow life down, think about it, and work out how you feel about things. Itl acts as a way for you to talk to yourself about what is important to you. Doing this lends strength to who you are as a person, and it allows you to deal with whatever life throws at you in a more positive way.

There are some general guidelines about keeping a journal that you may find useful to apply in order to lend it some structure:

1. Make a note of the date each time your write; it will allow you then to have a perspective of time as to when things happened and how you were feeling.
2. Write in the journal exactly when you feel like it. Do try to think about how you're feeling and write this down. Don't make yourself write if you're not in the mood; instead have a break from it until

you are. With this in mind, it can be beneficial to have a blank notebook rather than a diary. With a diary, you can feel pressured if there are lots of blank days, whereas if you're dating a notebook as and when you want to write in it, there are never any 'missing' days.

3. Be truthful at all times. There is no point in keeping a journal if you're not going to be honest. You're not writing for an audience; you're writing for you!

You may find it useful to have a set time of day or night that you write, when you won't have any interruptions. You may decide to write a certain number of pages or for a certain amount of time. But the key thing is to express everything you're feeling. I personally find that a set amount of time, with a timer set, is useful to me. Again, I'm not tied to writing for any longer than I want. If I chose 3 pages, some days I'd fill that quickly; other days I may agonize over writing them and it'd take forever. But, if I set aside a timed amount of 20 or 30 minutes a day and write as much as I can in that time, whatever I can get done is always acceptable to me. There's no target that I've missed by not having completed the 3 set pages. If I write 2 pages in that time, great. If I write 2 paragraphs, that's also fine. This is meant to be therapeutic and helpful to you, not something that you feel bad about, or beat yourself up about for not meeting a target.

If you are ready to talk to a counsellor, then try to find someone local. If you're in an educational establishment, there is often have a counselling department connected to them. They are trained to listen and gently guide you to make decisions. A counsellor will never tell you what to do or give you advice; that's not their role. But they will listen and help you to reach decisions that are right for you based on what you decide. You are in control.

This first half of the book has focused on creating the right mental state. In the second half of the book, you will learn tips and techniques that will allow you to have more control over your life.

Chapter 6 – Choose Your Friends Wisely

Often when we're growing up, people may try to guide you to stay away from certain people by saying that they were a bad influence, whether that's your parents or guardians, siblings, or other friends. They may have tried to encourage you to hang around with others because they seemed like nice people. You may have ignored their advice and done your own thing.

But, their advice was probably sound. There's a personal development expert, Jim Rohn, who states, "You become like the five people you spend the most time with. Choose carefully."

Have you thought about your close friend group?

These 5 people who are closest to you will either make you become a more social person who handles themselves with confidence, or else reinforce your shy, reserved behavior. It's inevitable that you will behave like the people you are closest to.

It's not their role or duty to behave in a certain way; you chose to be their friend. They will behave in the best way that they are able to.

People do, however, change over time; and so do friendships. If you have 'friends' who end up making you feel down, depressed, or fed up, then look closely at your relationships with them. If you have friends who frequently drag your mood down, consider carefully if these are people you want to spend a lot of time with. If they're not, then start to reduce the amount of time you spend together. You don't have to dramatically break off friendships - it doesn't have to be all or nothing - but you can spend more of your time with people who make you feel better. Life is short; you want to spend as much of your life as possible having fun, laughing a lot - real belly-laughs with tears streaming down your eyes - and looking back on fantastic memories of time spent in good company.

You can be very fond of someone, but still aware that if you spend too much time with them, it will drag your behaviour and activity into a bad place where you don't want to be. For example, if you have friends who drink heavily and party hard, then you may want to still be friends, but not spend every night of the week with them. Or else, if you're studying, you won't get good grades, and you'll probably damage your liver! Distancing yourself from people can be tough, but effective.

I'm not suggesting either that you drop your friends like a ton of bricks if they're having a hard time and need some support. Everyone, at times, will go through ups and downs in their life, and the help of friends can make those times a lot easier to deal with. Be supportive, listen, help out when you can, and try to help them have more fun and laughter. Just being a listening ear at times can help, even if you're unable to do anything practical.

There are friends who are cheerful, upbeat, and fun to be around 90% of the time, who have odd crises in their lives that they need support for. There are other friends who seem to have crises, illnesses, dramas, upset, depression, hatred, anger, and negativity 90% of their lives, and are only cheerful now and then. These type of people may genuinely have tough lives... but others seem to thrive on the drama, and drag people down at the same time. Have you ever had one of those friends or acquaintances who seem to have problem after problem, but regardless of what 'solutions' you suggest they try, they seem to poo-poo the idea of help, which wears you out and leaves you thinking, 'Why did I bother?'

It's not easy to change your friendship group. Some of the techniques discussed later in this book are easier. But, you definitely do need to be aware of who you spend time with and try to surround yourself with people who will help you become the person you want to be. Ensure you spend time with people who have similar life goals to you, and who are supportive and encouraging.

The Bond of Friendship

Most humans have something in them that makes them want relationships with others. We live in a social world, where we take on board the standards, lifestyle, beliefs, philosophy, and habits of the people around us. Most of us tend to like others who share things in common with us.

If you have a lot of friends who are not keen on socialising and find it hard to make small talk, it isn't really surprising that you think similarly.

Consider, however, how it would be if you had lots of friends who loved nothing better than the excitement of talking to new people and finding out all about them.

Would you have a different approach to life? Would you change your views? Would you see people differently?

This is how my life started to change. In the past, I daren't speak in social situations, because I was terrified of what other people thought. I expected them to judge me (as I judged myself with an inner-critic). But, the more time I spent with people who were social, the more I realised that talking to people was easy, and people weren't something to be scared of.

I watched my friends who were bubbly and confident start conversations and I saw that others enjoyed being spoken to and engaged in conversation. Most people want to be recognized by others and made to feel like they matter and are special and different. People who are extroverts focus on the other person, rather than how they'll be viewed, and by doing this they find it easy to talk to others.

When you have lots of bubbly people around you, you will, without being aware of it, pick up on their behaviour and techniques.

Try to Find People You Admire

As mentioned previously, don't just cull everyone from your life who doesn't seem 'useful' to who you want to be as a person. I do believe that every single person is special and has a strength, ability, and/or personal characteristic that makes them uniquely valuable. You are able to help them find their strength.

But, you can make a concerted effort to be around people you admire, and who you would like to follow in the footsteps of. There are two key types: real-life mentors and aspirational mentors.

Real-life mentors are people you know in real life. These are people who you see have characteristics that you would like to have yourself. They could be a manager at work, a teacher at school or College, a leader in the community, or a friend or colleague.

If you can't think of anyone, don't worry too much about this at the moment. There will be lots of like-minded people you can connect with, and towards the end of this chapter, I'll share a technique for how you can find them immediately.

Aspirational mentors are people who you respect and would like to be like. These people can be dead or living. They can live or have lived anywhere in the world. These can be inspirational people who may be an entrepreneur, an artist, a musician, an athlete, a public speaker, a politician, an author, or anyone else. There are no restrictions to whom you can select.

It's perfectly possible to learn the secrets of success from people who have walked that walk before you. It can be a quicker way to learn. Tony Robbins, a great motivational speaker, talks about standing on the shoulders of giants for a metaphor that shows you can learn from people in the past. You don't have to go through their mistakes and failures, but skip over these and get to the direct results much quicker. By reading about successful people, you can feel like you know them well and they're sharing their knowledge and experience with you. By emulating their techniques and habits, you, too, can become successful. It's like a short-cut to success. My plan for this book is that I can pass on my knowledge to you, of how I overcame shyness, so that you can learn the tips and tricks it took me years to master, in just a few hours of reading the book.

Section 2: Hints, Tips and Techniques

Chapter 7: The Strength of a Smile

So, you've made it through the first half of the book! Well done! The first half of the book can be challenging because it's about examining yourself closely. We all put up quite a front - even to ourselves. It can be tough getting past that to see your true self. But, only when you have found out exactly where you're at, what changes you would like to make, and how you would like your future to be, can you move toward change.

In this chapter, there will be tips and techniques that you can apply to real-life to break out of your shell and become much less shy and more sociable. These aren't theoretical; they have been officially tried by myself and I know that they work. And they have worked for others, too. This means that should you choose to employ the techniques here, they will work for you too.

When you're reading through the book, you can view this as your training.

When you're not physically reading the book, it's a case of putting things into practice. You need to keep trying these techniques. Not every one that you try will go perfectly smoothly. But, stay open to the fact that you WILL become more sociable, and that every time you practice your techniques, you'll make progress and become less shy.

The key here is to make steady progress towards your goal; you don't have to be an expert in socialising from day one.

Let's get on with learning the first technique...

Smile like a Sunbeam

When I started University, I had a class that started at 8am on four of the weekdays.

Many students aren't really early-risers by choice, and I was no exception.

But, I was also right at the start of the process where I was determined to become less shy, and I came up with a great idea for my first week at college.

From my accommodation to the class, I would pass, on average, 20 people. On one of the mornings, I chose to smile at every single person I walked past.

I did wonder whether people would think I was crazy for grinning at them, or think I was mentally subnormal, or a weirdo.

But, whenever I thought about these worries, I would consider the book, *Control the Crazy*, that I had learned from. I would then re-think and find the next passing person who I could smile at.

I was surprised that almost 100% of the people I smiled at smiled back at me. It's kind of contagious. You know, like when you hear the sound of someone laughing, it makes you smile or laugh, too; smiling is the same. If someone smiles at you, you want to smile back. It also made me think that it didn't cost anything to smile, but by being friendly towards someone, I had made another person's day brighter for a little while.

I did this for a few weeks and then added in another layer. I decided to start saying, 'Good Morning' to everyone that I passed.

I was amazed at the response I received from people. You may think, 'Well of course people will respond positively.'

But this habit transformed my life, because when I reached my early morning University class, I would feel positive and uplifted. This enabled me to carry on being social in class, and I had the strength to answer questions from the teacher and join in discussions. It's a much better approach to be as smiley, cheerful, and upbeat to as many people as you can, than to keep your head down and ignore everyone you pass. If I'd ignored people en-route, I wouldn't have felt as enlivened, happy and sociable; and this may have meant that in class, I continued to myself, kept my head down, and did not join in with class discussion.

I had gotten over some of my fear of talking to others by starting with a simple smile. That's all it took; and you can change your life in the same way.

Research Supports Smiling

This may seem like a very basic technique, but I promise you it's a fantastic way to feel immediately ten times more confident.

Research from various studies will also support that smiling has enormous benefits, even if you smile when you're not in the mood. I figure that it's not possible to feel negative and positive simultaneously. You can cheer yourself up a lot if you decide to smile when you're feeling a bit down.

There's a book called *Smile: Secrets of the Healing Power of Your Smile*, where the author, Elan Sunstar, talks about how what you're feeling emotionally is influenced by your physical health and vice-versa. If you change one, the other changes too. When you smile at someone, this stops any negative feelings and you'll instead start to think of positive associations where you feel happy. By feeling positive emotionally, you'll be healthier physically, too. You can see the converse effect also; if you're feeling down, and very frowny, this can mean that you're more susceptible to picking up cold and stomach bugs and you can feel generally quite lethargic. Making yourself smile can really turn things around when you may not feel like it. Plaster a huge grin on your face; and I can guarantee you will start to feel better physically and emotionally.

When we feel positive inside, we feel more able to speak to others in a confident way.

I would assume that, mostly, you have negative associations and feel awkward when you think about talking to others. So, it's natural you'd avoid doing so, because we want to distance ourselves from anything that's uncomfortable and do what is comfortable instead. You may find it easier to keep quiet and safe from putting yourself into uncomfortable situations. But, you've always done this, and to be frank, it's not really worked well for you so far, has it? If it had been going so great, you wouldn't be feeling fed up. You wouldn't be feeling awkward or uncomfortable. You'd just roll with it and be having a great, anti-social time. You wouldn't have picked up this book about overcoming shyness. The very fact that you are reading this book suggests that you'd like to be able to talk to others, and you'd like to be less shy. There is a phrase, which I've used before in this book, but it's a great reminder when considering change, 'If you always do what you've always done, you will always get what you've always got.' You can't continue behaving in a certain way and expect a different outcome; it's just not going to happen.

But, remember earlier in the book when we spoke about creating a change? It's necessary for you to make that change within yourself. The fastest way to do this is by smiling at others, even if you have to fake a smile.

Become a Morning Person

I now love early mornings and the opportunity I have to organize my thoughts during that time. I now wake up early, because it makes me feel good.

The part I dislike is that initial step out of a lovely, snuggly bed at 4am; but I can do this by training myself with a countdown from 3, which will be discussed later in Chapter 11.

I head immediately to the bathroom, and after brushing my teeth, head for a cold shower. Yes, cold!

I put a big smile on my face before the cold water hits me. I may look insane, but this motivates me. I gasp at the coldness, and it's the best feeling in the world. Cold water does have tremendous physical and mental health benefits; it'll do wonders for your circulatory system; it will make your skin glow and your hair shine; it will boost your immune system so you are less susceptible to colds and bugs; it will help to increase fertility, increase testosterone, and generally give you much more vitality and a sense of contentment. If you are a person who suffers from high blood pressure, then cold showers are not sensible, as they can make your blood vessels constrict. But, if you're otherwise healthy, you could try this and see how you feel. Cold water is great to wake you up and make you feel vitalized. Think of the difference too, when you're trying to work in a hot, stuffy room versus a cool room? When the room is too hot, you may start to either feel uncomfortable and sweat or else the heat can make you feel quite lethargic, drained, and devoid of all energy. It's not productive to be too warm. But, a cool room will keep you alert, focused and able to work. The cold water of the shower will make you really refreshed, alert, and able to think clearly.

In a similar manner to my physical morning shower, when I'm about to step into a social shower, where I may have felt a bit awkward and worried, I deliberately smile.

Smiling immediately reduces any anxiety. I can focus on what is happening around me instead of retreating to worrying thoughts in my mind; and I can focus on other people (rather than their opinion of me) and engage them in conversation.

You may consider forcing a smile a 'fake' way to live, and you may feel this would be a 'pretence' and a false, bizarre way to live. But, I promise you, after starting out with what may be a 'fake' smile for a few seconds, when you see real, genuine smiles returned to you, your smile will not be fake anymore; it'll spread and develop into a proper true grin. You'll make other people feel good by smiling; and this is a really positive thing.

Like Attracts Like

When you smile more at others and are more chatty with others, even in just a simplistic, greeting way, you will start attracting more positive people to you. People will start to want to talk with you. You won't have any concern over, 'What if I talk to someone and they don't speak back or think I'm odd, etc.?' People will make a beeline to speak with you and spend time with you. A happy person is a fun, positive, upbeat person to be around, and people are interested in happy people and what makes them behave that way.

Although, in the past, people talking to you may have worried you, you now do not have to worry about this. In Chapter 10 there will be some hints and tips for when people engage you in conversation and how to deal with it.

When you smile, people view you as an approachable, non-threatening, friendly person. Most people desire to protect themselves from being hurt or rejected. Without the need for you to even open your mouth to speak, smiling shows that you're a friendly person who does not want to hurt others. Let's face it – who would you rather approach? Someone who has their head down, shoulders slouched forward, who is not making eye contact, and is scowling? Or someone who is standing in an open, welcoming manner, whose eyes are bright and twinkling, and who has a lovely smile upon their face?

Prior to starting my smiling technique, often out of worry that someone would talk to me and I wouldn't know what to say, I would often hold my head low when I walked. I deliberately had a kind of blank expression on my face that gave nothing away. I was usually left alone by people; this appealed to me at the time, because for me, it was easier to be alone than to face my issues around socializing and risk being open and honest with others.

We can often make ourselves try to believe that we're happiest alone, not putting our thoughts or ideas out there and placing ourselves in a position of vulnerability. But, this isn't being truthful. When we connect with others, life is much more meaningful; it's much more fun when we smile at people and make connections. Memorable days in your life won't be the days where you successfully managed to avoid talking to anyone so they'll pass you by as unremarkable. Instead, they'll be the days you had an interesting conversation, threw some ideas around with someone, learned a new joke, learned a new recipe to try, perhaps made a new friend, or the first time you met your partner-to-be. All of these memorable days are based upon interactions and connections with others.

Smile Training

You do need to smile a lot every day. It's as important to keep practicing your smile as it would be to practice running if you were attempting a marathon. You can smile at any time around your house, initially, without having to smile at another physical person.

You can practice smiling when you take a shower, whilst you're hoovering, when you make a cup of tea, or when you cut the lawns. Smile at your pets. Start out by smiling around the house.

Try to use as many of your facial muscles when you smile as possible. Don't do this half-heartedly; really throw yourself into smiling, and use all your muscles to make a massive smile that wrinkles your eye lines, too.

If you live in the house with another person, whether it's your partner, parents, family, or room-mates, they may initially think you've gone a bit mad. Don't worry about them; instead lend them this book, and especially encourage them to read this chapter so they have a better understanding of what is going on. If they can understand and support you better, and even learn a few tips and tricks for themselves to apply, then it's all for the better.

When you're ready, you need to then be practicing these smiles out in public. There will be lots of opportunities for you to do this: when you go to fetch a newspaper or pint of milk; when you put the rubbish outside;

standing at a bus or train stop, and so on. Next, extend this smile to your work or school/college colleagues, with staff in shops, or at restaurants. With time, you will become known as the smiley person, the person who is always cheerful, always positive, and happy. And people love enthusiastic, happy people because they're a pleasure to be around. Happiness is contagious. It's motivating, inspiring, and will automatically make you appear a more confident person. A happy person appears in control, less stressed, with less issues and dramas.

It is perfectly natural that you may feel a bit out of your depth and uncomfortable at first. But, I can guarantee that other people aren't spending as much time thinking about you, or making judgements and critical comments about you, as you believe. People have better things to be doing; they're getting on with living their own lives and dealing with their own issues. This was another liberating moment for me, when I realized this. You need to believe this, too. Don't concern yourself with other people's opinions. Simply mind your own business, do everything in your own life to the best of your ability, and let other people worry about their lives, thoughts, and opinions.

If ever you start to worry about smiling and thinking you look silly, stop and thank your mind for its concerns. Then allow yourself to smile a big, massive grin once again! This can actually be quite a good technique for dealing with 'well intended' advice throughout life, too. If ever you feel someone is giving you advice that you didn't actually ask for or says things like "I tell you what you should do …" even if you think their advice is ridiculous, rather than get into an argument with them about it, you can thank them for their concerns, smile, and do your own thing! My Mum gave me that advice for what people will suggest when it comes to looking after/raising children, because everyone thinks they're the expert and knows best. So, just thank them, smile and nod, and go ahead and do things your own way. It's good advice for dealing with others, as well as your own negative thoughts.

Chapter 8 – Nonverbal Cues

Nonverbal cues are also known as body language. It's a key way we communicate with others, whether we're aware of it or not. It is said that 55% of what we communicate is through our body language, 38% through the tone of what we have to say, and just 7% of what we communicate is via the words.

So, if you worry greatly about speaking in front of other people and hope that you don't trip over your words or say the wrong thing, these statistics should take away a lot of your worry. The key thing you should be focusing on is your nonverbal cues.

There is a fabulous technique that I'll share with you; and it's easy to apply in social situations. When you do this, and adjust your nonverbal cues in this way, you will look and feel confident.

Ok, so here it is …

A-E of Confidence

By following these techniques, you will immediately be much more confident and animated in your stance and your conversation. It's a great hint for when you're meeting someone for the first time, speaking with a group of people, talking to your manager, or anywhere else. You need to recall A-E:

A: Adjust your body so that your shoulders are up and back - and stand firm.

B: Breathe deeply in through your nose and out through your mouth.

C: Clasp your hands together; this gives you something practical to do with them, so that you don't feel they're hanging there awkwardly. You won't be tempted to tap or fidget, and you'll look poised and in control.

D: Display your smile – place a big grin on your face.

E: Eye contact – ensure you look at people directly.

A-E has helped me so much in social situations that I didn't initially feel comfortable in. If ever I feel nervous, feel my hands starting to sweat, and begin to feel jittery, I remind myself of A-E and it helps to calm me down - and make me look much more confident.

Each of the A-E steps, only take a few seconds to achieve. I will now talk in a bit more detail about each of them:

Adjust Your Shoulders

When your shoulders stoop or slouch forward, this makes you look shy, indecisive, and can give a lazy appearance. It can make you look a bit shifty, too. People will sometimes refer to it as 'slouching.' People may assume that if you slouch, you're lazy, because they'll think if you can't be bothered to stand correctly with good posture, your other habits connected with work and life will be sloppy, half-hearted, and lazy too. This may be grossly unfair and untrue, but for people meeting you for the first time, or who do not know you well, this is the first impression they'll get of you. First impressions can shape how people perceive you in the future. They'll look for behaviour that reinforces their impression.

Now, whilst you may be the most honest, hard-working person in the world, your body language may send off different signals. There's an easy solution. Stand up straight, push your shoulders back and feel like you're having a good stretch of your rib cage. This will give you much more poise and will make you appear smart, confident, and like a go- getter.

I'll be perfectly honest and say that I find this habit hard to adhere to. My partner often reminds me to stand tall and not slouch. Whilst I found this a tad annoying at first, I know that my partner I right to point this out; and the reminders help me to focus on this and become better at it. If you would benefit from adjusting your posture, you could enlist the help of your partner, a family member, or a work colleague to mention it to you whenever they see that you're slouching. It will definitely help you down the line.

Not to mention the fact that having better posture has enormous health benefits, anyhow. Posture, i.e., the way that you hold and position yourself, not only makes you look confident and better, it has lots of key health benefits too. Having good posture can prevent you from developing pain in your back, neck, and shoulders. Good posture can prevent injuries and other health issues. Whilst spines have some curvature naturally, when you slouch, you're adding much more unhealthy curvature. You can cause your body to become misaligned. People often spend a lot of time and money with practitioners, having their body gently realigned. If you keep on slouching this can damage your spine and make it more likely to succumb to injuries. When your spine does not have good alignment, this places pressure on other joints, such as hips and knees. Your balance may be affected; you won't digest your food as easily; and you won't breathe as easily.

You can be aware of your posture, not only when you're standing up, but when you're sitting too. Ensure you keep most of your weight on the balls of your feet when you're standing, and aim to keep your head upright and level.

There is also something known as the Alexander Technique which could be well worth researching and investigating. Many celebrities and leaders follow this technique. It is all about finding balance, poise, good posture, and coordination, which runs through all you do in life. Having good posture can help you develop personally; it makes you more self-aware and mindful, and it will help you to more easily learn new skills and habits to transform your life. Practicing the Alexander Technique can prevent pain, injury, tension, and stiffness so that you move gracefully and with poise. It will give you the confidence to deal with everyday life stresses where you may previously have tensed due to nerves - for example, when speaking to someone on the phone or in person, having a meeting, or giving a presentation, etc. You'll learn techniques wherein you can identify stress and how to prevent yourself from reacting to these instances. Once you've learned the technique, it's yours to use for the rest of your life. You'll learn to have balance in your mind and body. It will give you more stamina; you'll learn how to relax; and you will have great clarity of thought. Singers and actors often learn this method because it can also help with breathing and vocal problems, too, making it great to help performers in music, drama and sports. It can also help people with their presentation skills and make you more eloquent. The technique can help throughout pregnancy and will generally improve your balance and coordination.

Breathe Deeply

Having a good posture and stance, with your shoulders back and a wide-open chest, will help with your breathing. Take a deep breath in through your nose; ensure you count to five before exhaling the breath through your mouth slowly (in a controlled way, not in an explosion of breath). As you're breathing out, imagine that all the stress, angst, anxiety, and concern you have in your body and mind is being breathed out of your body too.

Another way of getting rid of any anxiety, negative thoughts, and clutter that's in your head when you feel your head is too busy with thoughts, can be to imagine someone holding up an ice cube to your forehead. Imagine the coldness from the ice cube dissipating backwards as the ice melts, and trickling through your mind towards the back of your head, clearing out any of those hot, angry thoughts and replacing them with coolness and calmness. It's a nice visualisation technique that has helped me on many occasions.

If you are tense and coiled like a spring, this will show in your body language and the person you're speaking with, even if only subconsciously, will feel that you're uncomfortable. It can change your interaction entirely.

If you take two of the deep breaths discussed above, and perhaps apply the ice-cube technique to clear your mind, you will feel much calmer and more grounded and able to focus on people and what they have to say - rather than panicked and stressed.

Clasp Hands Together

Sometimes in a social situation, it feels as though my arms grow as long as the Mr. Men character, Mr. Tickle's, and I don't know where to place my arms or hands. I almost feel like I have as many arms as an octopus - and they get in the way! Having a stance where you position your hands makes you less self-conscious of them. You then won't fidget, put them in your pockets, pick at threads on your sleeves, tap your fingers, or twiddle your thumbs. It gives your hands a purpose.

If you're prone to twirling your hair or fiddling with your collar, or a ring or bracelet, once again these fidgety non-verbal cues will make anyone you're talking to subconsciously aware that you're feeling awkward. It may rub off on them and they can begin to feel a bit awkward, too.

There are some places where it's suitable to hold your hands. As a general guide, it can be advisable to have your hands near your chest when you talk and in your lap when you listen to others.

There are different types of ways that you can clasp your hands. You can have your fingers clasped flat to your hand or have them with finger-tips touching in a steeple position (which I personally think gives a calmer persona). But, the stance needs to be one that you feel comfortable with. You can practice this at home, in front of a full-body mirror, to see what you prefer the look of before trying it in public.

Display Your Smile

You've had plenty of practice smiling now, right? You need to keep smiling when you're talking with others. Make yourself smile and nod in the right places, too. This shows that you're friendly and open to their ideas. It shows you're listening to them and actively interacting with what they have to say. When you smile, it serves a dual purpose of giving you confidence and giving a boost of positivity to the other person, who will then respond to you well, too. If you don't smile and nod, the other person will feel quite disarmed and may worry that they're boring you or that you don't really want to be speaking to them. They may wrap the conversation up much quicker than they would normally have done.

Eye Contact

If you struggle to look people in the eyes, there's a way of looking like you are whilst not actually doing so. I'll explain this technique more in just a few moments. When you're in a conversation with someone, looking them in the eyes shows you're interested in them. They trust you and feel happy to talk to you. If eye-to-eye contact makes you feel a little uncomfortable, then try instead starting off looking at the person's nose, mouth, or the space in between their eyebrows until you feel better about looking them in the eye. This is great, because it's still around about the right place on their face. If you feel uncomfortable with direct eye contact at any point throughout the conversation, have a break and look at their nose instead.

So, you've mastered smiling and having a wonderful stance and calming, approachable body language. You're in a good place to try this out with people.

Chapter 9 – The Metre Rule

You are over half way to becoming super confident by having discovered how to control your body language. What we'll now focus on is actually speaking with people.

Over the years, you'll have become good at putting yourself in the background and away from situations where you have to speak with others. But, I 100% promise you, I've got some great news. It is MUCH easier to speak with people than what you've been worrying about. Once you start to do it, you will wonder why you've not done it much sooner. You will wonder what the big deal was. I'm not trivialising how you feel when you're shy, because believe me, I've had a lifetime of it. But, just when you cease to be and decide to change, life feels like you're really alive and living properly for the first time.

With just a few simple techniques, you'll be able to speak with anyone, from any walk of life, and engage them in interesting conversation. Sometimes we may worry that we're not of the same educational status or perhaps same class/social background as another person. This can make us hesitant to engage them in conversation, in case they think us foolish. Firstly, people who have been brought up well will have the manners to converse with you about most things. If there's ever anything you don't understand in a conversation, be brave enough to acknowledge this and ask the other person to explain. People generally like to teach others new things and to help them learn and understand. No-one will ever think you foolish for wanting to learn, because people love to teach and demonstrate their knowledge. My advice would be to never pretend you're knowledgeable on a subject that you're not; stick to what you know and can confidently talk about. And anything you don't know, take as an opportunity to learn about and ask questions. We'll cover more about the power of questions in Chapter 10.

A metre is 100 cm (or just over 3 foot). You need to pretend that you carry an invisible ruler or tape-measure of this length around with you. If anyone steps into this metre zone, you need to try to have a conversation with them. This is the new rule that you need to follow. Whilst you may be hesitant at first, I promise with time, you'll actually go out of your way to walk closer to people to get them to fall within your metre zone.

If you're a shy person, and have gone through life avoiding people deliberately, I know this may be initially terrifying to you. It's OK to be scared. But, please keep yourself open to change and to trying this out.

It is really easy to do.

Talk to Strangers

As children we're given the opposite advice of 'Don't talk to strangers' - and this is sensible advice for children to heed. But, when you reach the adult world, you need to talk to every person you get the chance to.

When you talk to as many people as possible, you open up the possibility that these people 'could' become good friends. You may find out that you have certain things in common with them, enjoy chatting with them, and want to spend more time with them. If you don't talk to people, it can make things at the workplace really tough, relationships non-existent, and you can become unhappy. Shyness really can impact you negatively. I know from experience. I once had a VERY small circle of friends - to the extent I had one real best friend and no partner for years. The people I spent a lot of my time with were my parents. And, whilst it's nice that we're a close family, there are certain activities that it's just much better to do with a group of friends instead, such as going to the cinema, going to parties, and fun days out. Certain things are more fun to do with people of a similar age to yours, without a generation gap. You need to chat with others to learn more about them and to make informed decisions about who you'd like to spend more time with and have as friends.

As human beings, we need to have meaningful connections with people. It can be a lonely, depressing life if you don't have friends. It's nice to have people you can call up and chat with on the phone. It's nice to have people you can go out for day trips with, share meals with, go to the cinema with, have cups of tea and cake with, play a round of golf with, watch a football game with, and so on. I want to assist you to be able to communicate with ease and express yourself.

What Will I Say?

Part of what stops us talking to strangers is our worry that they may think we're foolish. Or, we worry that they may not find us interesting. Or, we don't want to take up their time. We worry about what is the right or wrong thing to say.

There will be times in your life when you've wanted to speak with a person, but then you've become all flustered and can't think of a single sensible, coherent sentence to say to them. I've done this numerous times in the past when, due to nerves, my mind has gone so completely blank that I can't think of a single thing to say. I was once asked, "What music do you like?" and I couldn't think of a single band/group/singer. It was frustrating and ridiculous – I love music, but I couldn't even remember what CDs I had in the house or what I listened to on Spotify.

There's a great technique that will start you off with the Metre Rule; it's like a magic spell.

The Magic Spell

The magic spell is four special words, an incantation that you need to say out loud: "Hello, how are you?"

You're probably thinking to yourself, 'Is that all there is to it? Surely that won't work!!!!'

But, I promise you faithfully - and scientific research supports it - that this simple technique works!!!! So, this is perfect if you have concerns about what to say to start a conversation.

This technique above was learned by Vanessa Van Edwards, who I saw speak at a conference in Nashville. She studies people and their behaviour by profession; it's her area of expertise.

She has said that people wrack their brains for something which is unusual or funny to say, or something to try and make them look clever. But this line is 100% effective to start a conversation. It doesn't need to be any more complex than that. By keeping it simple, your comment isn't going to unnerve the other person, either. It's a relatively easy question that they'll be able to respond to.

So, if you say that line to anyone who is within a metre distance of you, you will soon start to have a lot of conversations. There are other techniques you can do when you're meeting people after that line which are also effective:

Shake Hands with Them

This isn't just to be professional or formal; there is a scientific explanation too. When you shake hands with someone, because your hands touch, you'll release oxytocin in your bodies, and this will forge a closer connection between the two of you. The other person will trust you more; it will form a bond. When we shake someone's hand, subconsciously we are working out whether we can trust them. If we believe we can, the brain releases oxytocin that tells us it is safe to trust them. At the same time as oxytocin, dopamine will be released, and this is like our reward and pleasure. Oxytocin makes us trust and become more generous, increases empathy, and will make us more understanding to others and allow us to see other people's perspectives.

This book won't go into the details connected to handshakes, though you could do further research on the Internet about this. But, ensure your hands are dry, have a firm grip that isn't too weak and floppy like a dead fish and also isn't overly aggressive. When you're shaking hands with someone, you're not trying to prove how strong you are. If the other person seems to be squeezing tightly as a show of strength, let them; it's obviously important to them for some reason.

Introductions

Try to keep your introduction brief, short, and sweet - and remember that you want to learn about the person you're speaking to. Here are some examples:

If you were at a gym you could say, "Hello, how are you? I'm XXX. What type of workout are you planning today?"

If you were in a coffee shop you could say, "Hello, how are you? I'm XXX. Do you have a particular coffee you would recommend?"

Once they reply, you can drive the conversation with more questions. There is a chapter, later in this book, which shows how powerful questions can be.

You'll be able to judge the best time in the conversation to shake their hand and make your introductions. Don't worry about saying the right words and remember that's actually a very small part (7%) of the whole communication. Follow the process as set out here.

Top Tip: It's much better to start a conversation than worry too much about trying to say the perfect thing.

One you've made your introduction and have got the conversation started, there are other hints and tips to keep that conversation going nicely.

Keep Smiling - and Nod, Too

If you're a person who is trying to be less shy, smiling and nodding will be your best friends. We can worry a lot before starting to speak with someone, as we think we need to control the conversation and have the right thing to say. Don't worry about this; just let it flow. If you're constantly trying to steer the conversation or planning what you'll say next, you're not truly listening and paying attention to what is said. Just ease into the conversation and you'll find it'll be much more natural and easy going. It's perfectly natural to have pauses in conversation and it is good to allow the other person to think and digest what has been said. Don't feel the need to fill every gap with babble.

When I speak with someone, I try to have an 80/20 rule, where I will get the other individual talking to me 80% of the time whilst I, myself, talk the remaining 20%.

This is because a lot of people like to talk about themselves. It makes them feel valued and appreciated, and like they're interesting and have knowledge to pass on that is useful to others, interesting, or amusing. I'm not just doing this to flatter their ego and butter them up; I genuinely believe this to be true, too. I think every single person has interesting things that they can share with you. When you're talking to someone new, you won't always want to open up and share your deepest thoughts immediately; but when you are comfortable in someone's company, it's much easier to discuss what you're thinking.

So, we need to make the person feel as comfortable as possible so that they're relaxed and at ease. Whilst the other person is talking, if you smile and nod, this will encourage them to keep talking. If you're a good listener, this will make you just as popular as a being good speaker - because people do love people who will listen to them and let them talk and throw ideas around.

If you apply your listening skills whenever you're in a social setting, you will be part of amazing conversations.

Ending the Conversation

When the conversation seems to be coming to its natural end, it's a good technique to enquire about the other person's future. This isn't intended to be really deep and meaningful (and not something like, "And where do you see yourself in five years' time?" That's more of an interview question), but simply something along the lines of:

"Do you have any plans for this afternoon?"

"Are you doing anything nice this weekend?"

This will allow your conversation to have a smooth finish, so that when you shake hands with them and say goodbye, you can add a personal touch of:

"It was lovely to speak with you, XXX. I hope you and your family have an excellent time this weekend at the Hockey game!"

Ending a conversation well is just as important as your initial impression. Taking the time to inquire about their plans, remembering their name, and making your conversation-end personal shows that you really care about them and were interested in what they had to say. You'll both end the conversation feeling good.

If you're chatting with someone and the conversation ends more sharply than you'd hoped for, don't worry or stress about it. There could be a million and one reasons why this has happened. It could be that they want to talk to others in the room; they may have a meeting at a certain time; they could need to use the toilet. Always keep smiling and, if you get the chance, let them know that you enjoyed the conversation.

If the person you've been chatting with seems like someone you'd like to keep in touch with, then a good strategy can be to ask if they're on Facebook. Lots of people are on Facebook or on LinkedIn, and it's a bit less personal than calling or texting a person. Especially if the person is the opposite sex to you, it can come across as a bit less like you're asking for a phone number for a date. If they are on Facebook or LinkedIn and do want to connect, it can be nice to pass someone your phone and let them put their own name in; it again lets the person trust you. For most people their phone is important to them, because it contains their contacts, photos, etc. Handing someone your phone shows that you are choosing to trust them.

If someone doesn't have Facebook or LinkedIn, or if they don't want to stay connected, don't be upset or take it personally. It won't happen often, but you can still be grateful for the conversation you've had; it's given you the chance to be confident and get some good conversational practice in.

Now, you've had a go at using the Metre Rule. You don't need to do this EVERY time that someone is within a metre of you; but please try to do it at least once a day. You'll be doing really well if you've started the conversation off and should feel very proud of yourself.

Chapter 10 – Asking Effective Questions

This is a key take-away from this book. If you only remember one thing from the book, please remember this: If you're wanting to try to keep the other person in a conversation talking for 80% of the time, so that you're able to listen and interact with them and be perceived as a person who is fun to have a conversation with, then you need to ask that person questions!

When I learned this tip, it truly did make a big change to my life. I carefully considered what it was that scared me about talking to people.

I figured out that for me, I was a bit scared of people - and I wasn't sure how to remain calm and avoid getting flustered in a conversational situation. But, when I asked the other person a heap of questions, this worked a treat. Asking questions allows you to deflect attention and the conversation away from yourself, onto them.

When you ask another person questions, you'll learn much more about them, as well as about a wide variety of topics. You'll learn about yourself, too. It's important to ask questions in a non-interrogation type way though; you don't want to bark questions at them aggressively in a rapid fire. It is better to use gentle, probing questions to show that you're interested and would like to find out more and to prolong the conversation.

When you ask a person questions, it's nice to try and find something that you both can relate to and have in common. If you feel shy and awkward, it can be because you think you're the only person who feels like this.

But, here's something to think about. All human beings do share a common trait. We all want to be accepted and loved, and we all have certain things we're afraid of. If you take the time to connect with a person and find out more about them, you'll discover that they probably have one of these areas of their life that they aren't as happy with as they could be. You are capable of connecting with anyone. I believe that every, single person has something interesting to share and talk about. Your mission, should you choose to accept it, is to find what their interest is, find something that connects the two of you, and try to expand this connection.

Questions are Powerful

In the past, I worked at a coffee shop. The mornings were often frantic, with people popping in to purchase teas and coffees for their morning commute to work. Regardless of how busy each morning was, I tried to ask each customer a question or pay each customer a compliment that would improve their day. This was a great technique to come across as friendly and interested, as well as offer good, personal customer service, getting to know my customers better and helping them to feel welcome and appreciated in the shop

One day, a gentleman in his thirties came in for his coffee with his children, who were boisterously running about. He looked very tired, probably due to caring for his children. As I passed him his coffee, I asked him, "What do you like best about being a Dad?" He hadn't been expecting the question and seemed initially a bit thrown by it. But after a few moments he replied, "Their love, which is unconditional. You just can't describe it."

He smiled and walked away after placing a tip in the jar. When answering the question, his face was filled with joy. The tip he left was very kind and appreciated. This exchange taught me something important - that when we ask another person the correct question, we can change their day. We can make them feel grateful for life even if they'd been having a momentary blip; they can feel noticed appreciated, and valued. My question to him probably took him away from how hectic the day was, how boisterous his children were being, and all the worries about the school run and issues that lay ahead for him at work that day - and instead reminded him about what was truly important to him and what he was doing it all for.

What Should I Ask?

How well you know a person will determine the level that a question should be pitched at. If you're meeting someone for the first time, you may not want to dive in with a really deep, meaningful question such as, "What's the meaning of life?" Conversely, if you've been dating someone for a number of years, you don't want to be finding out "What do you enjoy doing in your spare time?"

When you're just getting to know someone, here are some questions you could ask:

What are your interests?

How would you describe your family?

Do you have a favourite figure from history?

What's your background?

What do you enjoy most about being a parent?

If you were hosting a dinner party and could invite anyone from the past or present, who would you invite, and why?

If anything was possible with no constraints, how would you choose to spend your day?

Where in the world would you like to visit? Why?

Is there a book that changed your outlook on life?

These questions go beyond general introductory chit-chat and allow you to learn more about a person and who they really are, without making them feel awkward.

If you feel these questions are still too intense for you, there are some simpler ones here:

Are you employed? How do you spend your time?

Where did you study?

Where did you spend your childhood?

Do you have a favourite restaurant?

What's your favourite film?

Tell me about your best friend.

Where's the nicest holiday you've ever been on?

You don't have to worry about your exact words; what is far more crucial is that you're talking to a person - and you're asking questions that will get them thinking, talking, and engaging with you.

When someone replies to your questions, this sometimes leaves room to think of other questions that spring from the information they've told you. So, keep on questioning, listening, and commenting about their information. You can always have some standby questions at hand if you're worried about gaps in the conversation. But do listen actively and carefully, too. Don't worry about having to fill every gap or pause. Let the conversation take its natural course.

Actively Listen

Often when we're in a conversation, we can be focused upon trying to get our own points in or working out what our next comment or question will be. But, when we're doing this, we're not truly listening to the other person with our full attention. If you're a person who does this, really firmly work on damping down all the thoughts in your mind whilst you listen and concentrating on the other person and what they have to say. If you're busy thinking of what to say next, there can sometimes be a tendency to jump in and interrupt before the other person has finished speaking, which can come across as a little rude.

There are 5 things you can do in order to actively listen:

1. Give positive feedback to the person. You can do this in 2 ways - verbal and nonverbal. Verbal would include little affirmations such as, "Yes," "I agree," or, "I understand." Nonverbal feedback can include looking at them, nodding, and smiling.
2. Clarify any misunderstandings. If you don't totally understand what someone means when they're talking to you, you can ask them questions like, "Could you explain that?" When you ask questions like that, ensure it's clear that you're wanting to understand better and that you're not challenging them in an aggressive or sarcastic way. People don't mind explaining things; they want you to understand what they mean.
3. It can be a good idea to repeat back to the person what they've told you, but in your own words and phrasing. This allows them to see if you've understood what they're saying. You can start your comments with phrases such as, "If I've understood your meaning, you're stating that …." And then you can end with, "Is that correct?"
4. Don't interrupt the person as mentioned above; otherwise it can seem like you're rude, in a hurry for them to get to the point, or that you think you know better than them what they want to say. Other than making verbal feedback noises, or asking a question if you're unsure what is meant, try to listen in silence until the other person has finished speaking – even if this goes on for a while. Be patient, listen carefully, and drink in what they're saying. When you reply to them, try to ignore any heated emotions or emotional argument which can be used to sway you, and instead focus on logical, hard facts. By doing this, you're responding rather than emotionally reacting, which can often be quite knee-jerk. When you're emotional, you can often give a heated response, which you later regret when you've calmed down and have thought things through.
5. Be open, non-judgemental, patient, and neutral in your responses. When you're listening to someone, the key thing is that you understand what they want to say, not whether you agree or

disagree with them. When you keep yourself open, you'll be able to hear more of what they really mean and what they believe to be true. After this, you can talk about ideas.

The more you practice listening to people, the more you'll begin to hear the emotion in their words. This tells you much more than the words on their own.

Also look closely at what the person's nonverbal cues are. If the emotion in their voice doesn't seem to tally up with the words they are saying, then look at their body language, too.

If you've ever seen the TV show *Lie to Me* with the actor, Tim Roth, it's a brilliant programme that looks at micro-expressions and body language to determine people's guilt or non-involvement in crimes. Micro-expressions are about reading a person's face. Micro-expressions only stay on a person's face for a fraction of the time; they can pull a fake smile or create fake tears after this. You have to look quickly to see the micro-expression; it's involuntary and they can't help but do it. This could perhaps be the fraction of a smirk if someone is secretly pleased about something, even though they're pretending they're not. It could be the fraction of a frown if they were really hurt about something. In the programme *Lie to Me*, people would often be videoed - and it's only when the film was slowed right down in slow-motion that you could see the micro-expression. You can develop your skills in body language, following the tips in this book and using your powers of observation. There are seven key micro-expressions. These include surprise, fear, disgust, anger, happiness, sadness, and contempt/hate.

With body language, which is a bit more noticeable than micro-expressions, you can most likely tell those same seven categories by looking at someone's face, unless they're very adept at lying or acting. With other body language knowledge, you can look at someone's eyes. If someone's eyes are very dilated, this can be a sign of attraction or desire. If someone blinks a lot, they can be nervous, and this can be a sign of them feeling a bit agitated or distressed and uncomfortable. Or, you can look at someone's lips. If they bite their lips, this could be a sign they're worried.

If they purse their lips tightly together, this can be a sign that they've found something distasteful or disapprove of something. If someone covers their mouth with their hand, this could be to hide an expression, such as a smile or a frown.

It's possible for people to make various gestures and signals with their hands when they talk. Do be VERY careful to research hand-gestures, though, if you're in an international crowd and talking, because some hand gestures which seem innocuous to you could, in other parts of the world, have an offensive meaning. You could upset people without realizing. Gestures can be hard to interpret and the context does indeed need to be fully taken into account. For example, a clenched fist can at times represent anger and at other times can be used as a symbol for solidarity. Having a thumbs up or thumbs down can show that you either agree and approve or disagree and disapprove. The finger and thumb touching to make an O shape can mean 'OK' in some cultures. In others, it's offensive and means that you think the person is nothing. In yet other cultures, it's quite vulgar; so do be very careful who you use this around - or avoid it completely unless just with friends. Having two fingers in a V shape, can celebrate a victory or can be used to symbolize a swear word/gesture – again, use this with caution.

You can als0 analyse body language by looking at someone's arms. If they're crossed in front of them, this can show they're putting a barrier between you and them; it's quite a defensive gesture. It shows that they may be closed to anything you have to say to them because of this barrier. If someone puts their hands on their hips, this can be a symbol of being in control and may show some aggression. If someone is rapidly tapping their fingers, this could indicate impatience, boredom, or frustration because it's an outwards display of being a bit agitated and quite fidgety. You can also look at legs; if someone has their legs crossed, you can get an impression of how favourably they're viewing you based on whether they are crossed in your direction or away from you. It's typically more favourable if they're crossed towards you rather than away from you.

We've spoken a little about posture already, but how someone sits, whether they're keeping their body compact and tight, hiding their body with their limbs, or they have a more open posture, can let you know whether they're a bit unfriendly and anxious (closed) or friendly and open (open posture).

When you're speaking with someone new, be sure not to invade their personal space; leave a suitable distance between you and them. As a general rule, about 1.5 to 4 feet away is acceptable. You can judge how comfortable the other person feels as you're talking to them. If they step back a little, it's clear they need a little bit more space between you. If they step forward slightly, they're interested in getting to know you better. Some cultures differ in how they perceive personal space, with some cultures being happier standing very close to one another and others preferring more distance.

When you're next out and about, ensure that you speak to at least one person. Take on board where you are, try to find some common ground between you, and start talking to them.

It's perfectly fine if the conversation is brief and doesn't extend too much. This is about you having the confidence to speak with others and being brave enough to do something about it. Having been a very shy person myself, I can absolutely promise you that when you pluck up the courage and start doing this, firstly you'll see that people aren't that scary to talk to. Most people are courteous and friendly and only too happy to talk. But, once you've chatted, even if it wasn't the most ground-breaking conversation ever, you'll feel very proud of yourself for having initiated the chat.

Chapter 11 – The Secret Recipe

You may have previously heard about some of the techniques in this book. It can be useful to have a reminder sometimes to make the idea seem worthwhile. Other times, we need the idea put to us in just a slightly different way that makes it make sense to us.

In this book, I've given you hints and tips that have been used by thousands of people over the years, which have helped them to become less shy and express themselves with more ease.

This last technique, however, you may never have heard of previously - and this is the secret recipe you need to bring all of this together and make it work.

You may in the past have known how to do something, or what you should be doing, but haven't done it. (Think of diets/exercise regimes for instance – it's not rocket-science, but is much harder to do).

How many times in the past have you thought about what you 'could' be saying to someone who looked like an interesting person, but instead you remained quiet and reserved and didn't speak?

The moments where you prevent yourself from doing things end right now.

Stop Sabotaging Yourself

You may find a lot of helpful videos on YouTube that could be immensely useful to give you information or change your approach to life. In one video called 'How to Stop Screwing Yourself Over' by Mel Robbins, she emphasizes that we already know what we want. But, when we're thinking about acting on something, our emotions and thoughts battle with one another - and it's our emotions that win. It's hard to talk yourself into an action, no matter how logical it may seem, when you're scared.

So, for example, you may have battled with thoughts such as:

'They look like a nice group of people over there who I'd like to sit with and chat, but I daren't go and speak with them.'

Or, 'I have some ideas I'd like to share with people at work, but I don't have the confidence to speak out.'

Or, 'I'd like to ask that person on a date to the cinema, but what if they say no?'

Emotions and feelings can be important, and they can work well for us or work against us, depending on whether they make us act, or we fail to act because of them.

So, you may know what to do; and you have your motivation for why you want to do it. But, that isn't always enough to spur you on to action. There is, however, a solution.

In the video mentioned above by Mel Robbins, if you want to act on an aim, you MUST do this within 5 seconds, or else your emotions will take over and will stop you acting.

What you can do to force yourself to move is start a 5 second countdown. So, for example, if you'd just been to a gig of a musician you liked and, after the show, they were mingling among the crowds chatting to people, when you see them, you have...

5... 4... 3... 2... 1... to say "Hello. How are you? My name is X."

If you're in a workplace meeting and your manager asks, "Does anyone have anything to add about how we could tackle the X issue....?" you have...

5... 4... 3... 2... 1... to start speaking up and sharing your ideas.

There will be lots of opportunities in a day where you can apply this rule to force yourself to act, become less shy, and start expressing your thoughts.

Ralph Emerson speaks about how people who act are powerful; whilst those who do not move and do something are powerless.

So, you need to stop analysing and dwelling over every aspect of your life and just do things, live life, and act exactly how you want to. You start to become powerful when you make the effort to just do things.

You could spend years of your life, or indeed your whole life, just reading self-help books, listening to podcasts, watching seminars... and still nothing much has changed in your life, until you make the decision to change and act. You need to be courageous and take that first step. If you just keep waiting until the perfect moment, you'll keep waiting forever.

So, this secret recipe can change your life, because it's all about you physically acting very quickly - within 5 seconds.

Twist to the Recipe

When I tried the 5 Second Rule strategy of knowing I wanted to act, just counting down 5 seconds, and ensuring I had acted within this time, I got brilliant results immediately.

I managed to keep getting up at 4am and jumping into a cold shower. I countdown to get in the shower.

If I was out and about at the shops and wanted to ask someone I'd not met before a question or pay someone a compliment, I would start the 5 second countdown.

If I'd been putting off making a telephone call at work, I would start the countdown.

But, I did make a small tweak and twist to the recipe.

I felt that counting down 5 seconds was a bit too long. It was long enough for my brain to start going into a panic - and I'd have time to start talking myself out of things. So, I cut down my countdown to 3 seconds and this worked much better for me.

I'm not perfect every single time with any of the techniques I've suggested in the book. I do still feel afraid from time to time, and occasionally I won't speak to someone when I wish I would. But, if these instances occur, I don't let it stress me out too much, and I don't dwell on it and think about it for ages. Because becoming less shy is something which I've committed to work at for life, and I'll gradually keep on improving.

So let's try out the exercise right now. You need to think of something that you've been procrastinating about. What is something that you've had on a 'to do' list but still haven't actually got around to doing? It could be that you keep saying to a friend, "We must catch up for coffee," but then you don't. Or you could owe someone an apology that you haven't given them yet. Or, there could be part of your house that you've been meaning to sort out, such as a drawer, a cupboard, or a room.

Once you've focused on what it is that you should have done, put down this book and start your countdown, whether that is from 5, or 3, whatever works best for you, to get you to act:

3... 2... 1...

If you start to think of all the excuses under the sun for why you shouldn't do this, put those out of your mind and start your timer once again. Don't waste another minute of your life; just get things done. When you're next in a social situation, try this technique as often as you can.

Using this technique will allow you to achieve immediate results and start having meaningful conversations with others. It's a call to action which has an immediate result. It stops you procrastinating, stops you putting things off until 'someday' – because you need to act now to change your life for the better.

Chapter 12 – Lifelong Learning and Development

Have you tried the 5 or 3 Second Rule? How did you get on? What are your thoughts and feelings about it?

If you haven't yet, then again, put down this book and do it right away!

This book is meant to encourage you to make changes and act - so that you can become more of who you truly are.

Assuming you have made some of these changes and used some of the other hints and tips within this book, we can move on. This book is coming to an end shortly.

There is No End

When I read *Control the Crazy* for the very first time, it changed my life. I have since gone back and read that book many more times. You can't always take everything in the very first time you read it. Also, it was helpful for me to have the frequent reminders within the book to take on board the ideas and techniques within it. It encouraged me anew, each time I read it, to stop feeling down and negative and to push out any worries or concerns in my mind.

I truly believed that the contents of the book were highly valuable and relevant to me, to such an extent that if there was anyone else whom I felt could benefit from the book and seemed interested in the ideas, I would share my copy of the book with them. I started looking for more books filled with similar strategies.

Since reading that, I have read over 200 other books and have listened to thousands of hours of audio books on a wide variety of topics, including self-help, human development, sociology and psychology. I prefer the term 'self-discovery' to self-help.

It isn't my intention to boast about how well read I am in this topic, but instead to profess upon you how beneficial it can be to constantly learn and develop on a journey to self-discovery through books, videos, podcasts, audio-books, seminars and so on, so that you're constantly keeping your mind open to new techniques. It empowers you to transform your life.

When you read a book or hear an audio-book, it is as if an idea has been planted within your brain. When you act upon any of the suggestions within the book, this allows growth and development. You do need to act, though. Actions are like food and water to the seeds, and they won't grow and develop without action. When you harvest your crop, it feels incredible. You'll be so proud of yourself and your achievements.

I do hope that this book has been useful to you, so that you will re-read it and share the ideas within it (or the book itself) with friends and family so that they can benefit, too. I also want you to discover lots of other authors and speakers who discuss similar topics, so that you're constantly expanding your knowledge and skills, and gaining technical abilities to deal with any issue life throws at you.

You need to keep on learning to stay alive.

I was never a great reader when I was at school. I always used to opt for the easier route of summary books that told you the gist of what was happening.

I now have confidence and contentment; and II feel good about myself. I discovered that learning doesn't have to be just academic and rote memorization; learning can be learning more about who we are, daring to be who we are, and feeling stronger to be able to be less shy and express ourselves. In the first half of this book, you've learned a lot about yourself, and it can be tough to be totally honest. But, it's necessary so that you can move beyond this, to change and make great improvements to your life.

What Now?

I would like you to be committed to lifelong learning and development, so that you can constantly strive to develop and grow as a person - and be who you truly are.

Think about how exactly your life will be when you're no longer shy. Who are you? What will you do? Where will you go? Is there a difference that you will make to the world?

We don't 'just' want to focus solely on becoming less shy, because there's more to life than that.

Life is short; there are no reruns or second chances with it. You don't want to live just a middling, average, run-of-the-mill life. You want your life to be extraordinary! I know that you have things that are very special about you that set you apart from other people. You are talented, you are able, and you have a gift that you could share with the world. Dare to be yourself. Dare to live life as you want to. You will constantly throughout life have people telling you how you 'should' be and you need to be who YOU want to be.

Be you - exactly as you are. You are you; you are special; you are perfect exactly as you are. Live a life that you're proud of. I believe you're capable of anything that you put your mind to.

Bonus

You have everything you need within this book to become less shy and express yourself fluently and with ease. If there are moments when you need to push yourself into action, you now know the countdown from 3 technique, which will force you into action.

Before this book ends, I wanted to share a final story with you. This transformed how I live my life, and I feel certain your life could be changed too.

When I was younger, my dad would drive me to school. This became a bit of a tradition. The journey was only approximately 12 minutes, and during that time, I felt I could talk to my dad about anything. This could be school, relationships, sport, politics, or life in general. It was a very open space, where I could say anything. My father was definitely an adult. He wasn't like one of my friends my age; but he was also my confidant.

When we reached the school gates, he would hand me some money to go towards lunch, give me a hug, and then say, "Be the best person you can be today!"

As I was growing up throughout my teenage years, this seemed like a warm and fond saying from my dad, but I hadn't fully realised the significance of the words.

A lot of time has passed since my school days. Life is challenging at times, with various hurdles in the way. I look back very fondly on that time spent with my Dad, and I have frequently thought of those words.

If we constantly strive each day to 'Be the best person we can be,' we need to be fully aware of who we truly are as people. We need to be thankful and appreciative for the good things in life that we have. We need to be calm and content. We need to be totally truthful to ourselves and others. If we make an error, we need to own up to it and try to resolve it. We need to keep humility, be as loving as possible, find new adventures to keep us challenged and intrigued, push ourselves beyond our comfort zones to stretch and grow, and we need to try to make a difference to other people's lives, too.

Thank you for reading this book and letting me try to help you on your journey to becoming less shy and having the ability to express yourself. I hope that there's at least one thing you can take away from this book that has made a difference to you. Please feel free to share the book with your friends and family so that it can help them to understand you better, and perhaps pass on some hints and tips to them, too.

Be the best YOU that you're able to, today and ever after.

Good luck and best wishes!

www.ingramcontent.com/pod-product-compliance
Lightning Source LLC
Chambersburg PA
CBHW071458080526
44587CB00014B/2145